Your Home Color Guide

Making Color Work

ASK THE HOME COLOR WIZARD℠

VIRGINIA CARR

To Pat
Best wishes
and colorful
days! Virginia

Smart Home Moves® Press

St. Clair Shores, Michigan 48080

Published by Smart Home Moves® Press
Post Office Box 104
St. Clair Shores, Michigan 48080

Making Color Work
Ask the Home Color Wizard[SM]
By Virginia Carr

Book design and production: Maria Catalfio

Farmhouse photograph: Diane Lahr
    ©1993 Virginia Carr

ISBN: 0-9640510-1-x

Acknowledgments

A special thank you to my associates, friends and family who gave their time, expertise, and unending support that helped turn an idea into reality. To each and every client I've worked with, thank you, too, for the questions. Here are the answers. This book is for you.

Thank you Glenn Haege for inspiring me to write this book.

With love and appreciation
to my parents
Sam and Mary
and my daughters
Kathleen, Karen and Kristin
for making my dreams come true.

"SAWDUST AND SANDWICHES"

"From the time I stood knee-high to a hammer on end, I was 'on the job.' The foundation for this book began long before I knew it."

I can't count the times Mom packed my brother and me into the car to take Dad a warm lunch and eat with him at the construction site. We watched him build many a home, from pouring the footings right on up to setting the last shingle. We not only learned how to pound a nail without hitting our fingers, but also how to use a dust pan and broom. Yet we always found time to play hide-and-seek in the empty rooms. The most fun was parading around with long curly wood shavings on our heads and building skyscrapers out of blocks of 2"x 4"s.

Shaped by my talented artistic mother who first put a crayon in my tiny hand, and my father who put a hammer in the other, I was beginning my designing career.

To this day, the sights and sounds of construction — buzzing saws, the rhythm of busy hammers, the sweet smell of freshly cut lumber, and the aroma of home-baked bread — sweep me back to those family picnics perched on Dad's favorite sawhorses.

After receiving a teaching and Bachelor of Arts degree from Marygrove College in Detroit, Michigan, my graduate education in color and design continued while juggling three energetic daughters.

For twenty-some years now, my career as an interior designer/builder has taken many forms, yet all linked to the building industry: designing and building homes, co-authoring and producing a weekly Builders Home Show on NBC in Detroit, and producing infomercials on FOX 50, also in Michigan.

Smart Home Moves® was created for the do-it-yourselfer. It is a color coordinating and home improvement consulting service. It provides on-site help for people who are building, moving or improving their home, apartment or office spaces. Better known as the "Color Wizard," I conduct *Ask the Home Color Wizard* workshops and seminars, and write newspaper articles and advice columns to help people get more home out of their house with color. Beautiful homes are no accident — they are well planned.

For additional information on seminars or books contact,

Smart Home Moves®
P.O. Box 104
St. Clair Shores, Michigan 48080

FORWARD

One day you see an old storefront being painted a modern color. The next day a new awning in a contrasting color is added. Suddenly, an old, dilapidated building looks new and inviting. You decide you better go into the store and check out the merchandise because it might be interesting.

Virginia Carr, the "Color Wizard," is here to tell you that you can do the same thing to your house, inside and out. She calls it *Making Color Work.* I like the idea because using a paint brush is easier than swinging a hammer and a lot less expensive. I've had Virginia on my radio show and have been impressed with how she can give listeners advice on how they can make rooms bigger, smaller, cooler, quieter, almost anything-er. And she does it all with color.

Now, Virginia's vast color knowledge has been condensed into one very easy-to-read book. I think it's a must for anyone who is thinking of redecorating, remodeling, building, buying or selling a house, or even just has one little room that isn't quite right. It's also a great book for anyone who is renting a house or apartment. In other words, I think this is a great book for everyone.

This book is well written and laid out so that it's easy to under-stand. It is going to have a permanent place in my library. I hope it finds a place in your home, too.

Glenn Haege
America's Master Handyman
Southfield, Michigan
June, 1994

COLOR DOES NOT STAND ALONE
SEE YOUR HOME IN A NEW LIGHT!

Has a gallon of paint ever mysteriously changed color in the trunk of your car on the way home from the store? Are you afraid of color, and bored with beige? If you have ever had a wallpaper headache, lost your shirt or painted yourself into a corner, this book is for you. Now you can amaze yourself and your friends by performing color magic on your home without spending an extra penny.

From the moment the first rays of light kissed the earth, the gift of color was ours. Nature's colors surround us from sunrise to sunset. Its ever changing colors are a feast for our eyes. Color warms and enriches our lives, lifts our spirits, and weaves joy, pleasure and comfort into and around our homes. Its magical power can affect us both mentally and physically — whether we know it or not, because it is tricky. When it comes to home improvement and decorating our homes inside or out, we can't even begin a project without thinking about color.

Sooner or later we are all faced with making a color decision, big or small. Whether it's a single blanket or towel, a truckload of bricks, six squares of shingles or a couple of shutters, or cabinets, carpeting, hardware, paint, even the kitchen sink, you can't "cut corners" when it comes to color. Putting the right colors in the right places not only makes you feel good — it increases the value of your home.

America is getting a face-lift and we are doing-it-ourselves. On the average, over 40 million people move each year and some 30 million remodel their homes. To accommodate this growing trend, thousands of home improvement centers and decorating shops have popped up all over the country. And you are all asking the same questions: "Where do I begin; what color goes with what, where and why?" With so many products to choose from in a variety of colors, it's enough to give a chameleon a major migraine.

This book is the tonic to soothe your nerves, answer those questions, and show you how to turn dull spaces into exciting places in a "snap" like a pro. By the time you finish reading it, you will see and feel color as you never have before. You'll be able to defy the laws of gravity, levitate your ceiling, and even make furniture appear and disappear with the swish of a brush. You will be able to move walls without a hammer or crow bar, change the mood of a room from chilling to charming and even control the appetites of your unsuspecting dinner guests — and you'll do it all with color.

No, you don't have to be a magician, a Vincent Van Gogh, Leonardo Da Vinci, a renowned designer or even a "color wizard" to have a beautiful home — you just need to know their secrets. And no, you don't need to take out a second mortgage. Put away your check books because the best and biggest news is that color is **free!** It is within the reach of every budget. Color is part of everything we purchase whether we realize it or not. The choice is up to you. It costs no more to select things with lively colors that harmonize, than it does to select those that are boring or end up fighting each other. However, color can play tricks on us and you can't afford to be in the dark about that. Its most powerful accomplice is light.

Mistakes are easy to make, hard to live with and costly to change. So when it comes to your cottage, your castle, your place of business, or anywhere in between, make it right with color and light. This book will help you learn how to make color work for you by controlling the optical illusions that light creates. You can rely on it from start to finish. It takes the mystery and fear out of using color. The tools, tips, tricks and ways to avoid the traps of color are at your fingertips.

You are holding in your hands a book of color instructions. Use it for every purchase you make — it will not only save you precious time, but thousands of dollars as well. Keep this book handy in your toolbox, glove box or trunk of your car. Whether you are working on a shoestring or champagne budget, your living space need not be costly, but it can be expensive-looking, with proper use of color.

Like magic, you can do it yourself, whether you are painting a single wall, selecting hardware or building a brand new home. Instead of your dollars ending up in a money pit, you'll find a pot of gold at the end of the rainbow.

As you stand amidst the rubble of your unfinished project or new home, overwhelmed by the countless number of decisions, relax! Just imagine yourself in the Emerald City, like Dorothy in "The Wizard of Oz." Hold this book tightly in your hands and make a wish. Click the heels of your comfy sneakers, your heavy work shoes or your sparkling ruby red slippers and repeat... "There's no place like home, there's no place like home, there's no place like home sweet home . . ." and like magic your dreams can come true in any of the colors you love. For most of us, our homes are our biggest lifetime investment. It only makes sense to enjoy them while protecting their value and maintaining their appearance. What you select today will live with you for many years. Make every move a *Smart Home Move!*

YOUR HOME COLORING
GUIDE

For Getting Color Right,
An Investment for the Future

Stop! Before you begin scraping, sanding, or steaming your walls, chipping away at the old paint; before you drive another nail or make plans for building a home. Don't even think about starting a project or even purchasing a simple table lamp, until you read the following information carefully. It will help you understand what goes with what color, and why.

Never before has such an important guide been published.

It seems we get instruction manuals with everything: from power tools, appliances and automobiles, to leisure toys, VCRs (which still elude me) and every home improvement product or material . . . except color.

We can walk on the moon, list the genus and species of everything under the sun, know the habits of the birds and the bees, heal our bodies with beams of light, and yet when it comes to color in our own backyard, kitchen or rooftop, most of us are baffled and afraid to make a move.

Warning! To reduce the risk of losing your shirt, painting yourself into a corner or ending up in the red, do not shop without this guide. **Don't loan this book out** — you may never get it back. Rather, hand out one of the handy order forms at the back of this book or give one as a gift.

For your convenience the back cover displays the most important tool for *Making Color Work: a color wheel.* That's where it all begins. Each wedge of color has been numbered like a clock for easy reference. You'll also find a handy ruler on the back cover, and dozens of "wizdoms" throughout the book. Watch for this symbol in the margin:

Section 1 is *The Personal Side of Color.* It will *Tune You In and Turn You On to Color* by showing the personalities of different colors and some fun stuff to pinpoint the colors you like and why.

Section 2 opens your eyes to *The Tricky Side of Color;* its special effects and how to remodel with color instead of a hammer.

Section 3 is about *Colors That Say Home to You.* Dress your home to suit your fancy! An overview of different styles and themes for you to consider.

Section 4 provides *Home Color Plans:* "What Goes With What" and the how-to steps, tools and tips to spruce up a room or make plans for a brand new home.

Section 5 is *A Quick Review of Fifty-Nifty Tips* for people on the go.

Section 6 is *Your Coloring Workbook.* This section follow the steps in section 4. It includes space to record measurements, draw floor plans and pages for collecting pictures, paint chips, fabric samples and swatches.

This color guide belongs to:

_____

Address _____

State_____ Zip_____

Phone_____

12

COLORWIZE WORDS

1. **A COLOR WHEEL** is a rainbow in the round, organized to define the relationship of one color to another. Each wedge contains a tint and shade of each color. It is the basic starting point of understanding color and a reference to easily develop your color schemes. See Section 4 for plans of what goes with what.

2. **HUE** is another name for color, as is chroma. **TONE** refers to hues to which gray has been added to give them a misty or smoky look. This changes the intensity.

3. **INTENSITY** is the brightness or dullness of a color. Hot pink and kelly green are two bright colors. Adding a gray pigment reduces the bright values and dulls the color down. Examples are dusty rose or olive green.

4. **VALUE** refers to the lightness or darkness of a color. These are referred to as tints and shades.

5. **A TINT** is a color that has been mixed with white. Also referred to as a pastel. Powder blue is a tint. The more white in a color, the more light it reflects

6. A SHADE is a color that has been mixed with black. Navy blue is an example.

7. WARM COLORS include red, yellow or orange. They represent half of the color wheel, and are referred to as daytime or sun colors. These colors make you feel warm and toasty.

8. COOL COLORS are green, blue and purple and represent the other half of the color wheel. We associate them with evening colors and coolness, and they tend to be more relaxing.

9. NEUTRAL COLORS, sometimes referred to as the "uncolors," are black, brown and white. They are easy colors to live with and can be a part of any color scheme. Their names range from beige and taupe to charcoal and off-white.

10. SCHEME is an organized color plan. Look at the color wheel on the back cover to better understand these three most common schemes: *monochromatic* (which means using one color wedge and any of its tints and shades); *neighboring* (using two or three wedges next to each other on the wheel), and *contrasting* (using wedges directly across from each other). See Section 4 for details.

11. PALETTE refers to the actual intensity, tints and shades of colors you select to fit into any of the three schemes.

12. A COLOR PLAN is a record of room measurements and collection of colors, samples and swatches arranged in a folder to use as your guide for a project.

You will find all colors in a variety of values and intensities. Be careful mixing muted colors with bright colors in the same scheme. One can make the other look faded or dirty.

13

12 MONEY-SAVING
"SLIGHT OF HAND"
T   R   I   C   K   S

Put away the power tools! See how much money you can save with the swish of a paint brush and a few color tricks. Let these optical illusions do the trick:

1. **Instead of adding a fireplace,** warm up your room by painting the walls with one of the warm colors: red, yellow or orange .

2. **Paint your room with green,** purple, or blue before you invest in a room air conditioner to make it cooler.

3. **Raise or lower a ceiling** without a demolition crew. Simply use light colors. They visually lift a ceiling because they reflect more light. Darker colors do the opposite.

4. **Expand the size of a small room** by painting the walls with pastels or a light version of beige, gray or off-white.

5. **Before you demolish** unsightly architectural features like a steam radiator, woodwork or an unwanted bookcase, swish them away with a paint color that matches the walls.

6. **Down-size or square off** a room without adding a partition. To make it more cozy, paint it a deep shade. To square off a room or shorten a long hallway, paint the two short walls a shade deeper than the two long walls.

7. **Brighten up a windowless room** or one that has a small window. Paint the ceiling white and the walls a light color. Then add a mirror to reflect more light, a

brighter light bulb, and a translucent lamp-shade.

8. Put away the sandpaper. Play down heavily textured or uneven walls with defects by using a flat, non-reflective paint finish. The more glossy the finish, the more attention it draws.

9. Instead of using a power saw to cut down the size of furniture that seems too large for the room, either re-cover it, paint it to match the color of the wall, or paint the wall to match the piece.

10. Expand the look of an entire home by weaving a light color throughout. The most effective way is to paint your walls a light color. Keep the floor coverings the same color and ditto for all the wood work. The common coordinating denominator is color, no matter what material is used for floors or walls. Bring in blending colors in the furnishings and accessories.

11. To expand the exterior look of your home, paint out vertical distractions, like contrasting down spouts or a garage door that overpowers the house. Keep those unattractive features close to the color of the facade or shell of the house.

Mature trees can add up to 15% to the value of your home.

12. Add curb appeal and thousands of dollars to the value of your home by making it more attractive with a little paint. Begin with a grand entrance. The front door is an important focal point. It is the welcoming center of your home. Paint it a *muted* contrasting color to your facade. Paint shutters the color of your roof. Perk up the home by adding more color in your flowerbeds

10

COLOR TRAPS TO AVOID

Mistakes are easy to make,
hard to live with and
costly to change.

1. Selecting colors and patterns from postage-stamp size samples.

2. Making snap decisions without considering the light source in your home.

3. Shopping when your home is starved for color, thus making hasty decisions without a color plan.

4. Purchasing something just because you fall in love with the name of the color or because it's the trend.

5. Getting color advice from well-meaning people who do not live under your roof.

6. Color intensity increases with quantity. Remember this especially when painting your walls. Select something a little lighter than your first choice.

7. Not understanding the special effects color can create.

8. Mixing "misty" colors with pure colors (those in the middle circle of the color wheel with no white, black or gray pigment) in the same room. One can make the other look dirty.

9. Not considering the durability, finish or maintenance the colored object or surface requires.

10. Shopping without this book!

THE
ABC'S
OF COLOR

Always ask yourself these questions before you make a color selection for anything!

A

What do I want the AREA or item to do?

This includes: wall coverings, windows, woodwork, fabrics, furniture, cabinets, hardware, laminates, floor coverings or accessories, bricks, shutters, shingles, gutters, garage doors, flowers, shrubs and trees.

B

Do I want it to BLEND?

Blending whatever it is to its background color, or matching it to its surroundings, tones it down and makes a quiet transition from one thing to another.

C

Do I want it to CONTRAST?

Contrasting colors are lively. They create focal points. They do all the opposite things that blending does. They draw attention and make things stand out to be noticed.

Blend or contrast?

Cover each half
to see the
difference

TABLE OF CONTENTS

Section 3: Colors That Say Home To You

Section 4: What Goes With What and How?

Section 5: Fifty-Nifty Tips at a Glance

Section 6: Your Coloring Workbook

1
THE PERSONAL SIDE OF COLOR

How To Tune In And
Turn On To Color

THE PERSONAL SIDE OF COLOR

Response to color is both inherited and learned, and varies according to such factors as sex, age, education, ethnic and cultural backgrounds. Past experiences affect our likes and dislikes in color as do our peer groups, the climate in which we live, and regional attitudes.

— Wagner Institute for Color,
Santa Barbara, California

There's a purely personal spin on the color wheel which we need to take into account when feathering our nests. It's very important to become aware of how we *perceive* colors and how they *affect* us. From the time we were tiny children, for instance, we learned that fire is hot and ice is cold, so naturally when we see reds, yellows, and oranges we associate these colors with warmth and activity; and we see blues, greens, and purples as less active and cool. This perception affects the visual temperature of things in varying degrees, from person to person, and is influenced by how light or dark the color is and the depth of its intensity.

We also seem to associate light-tinted colors with casualness and see dark shades as more formal. Our mood can definitely be swayed by what we personally associate with a color. It can make us feel happy or sad, mellow or edgy. Listed here are some common responses. Bear in mind that these color families include all values and intensities of colors and any of their given names, such as cranberry, mustard, scarlet, heavenly blue, shrimp, or olive. The more intense, or deep, the color, the stronger the response. The lighter the color, the less intense the response. Staying aware of your personal side of color will enable you to make an area feel good as well as look good, and that equals comfort.

COLOR IS WHAT COLOR SAYS TO YOU

Have you ever stepped into a home, office or public place and felt uncomfortable? Did it seem cold and unfriendly? Or was it charming and warm? It's quite possible it was the colors, not the people. See what color says to you.

WARM COLORS
Red, yellow, and orange

Warm colors are associated with things that "feel" hot or warm, sometimes called "daytime" colors. These are aggressive colors, the attention-getters.

RED
Danger and romance

- The color of blood, courage, and sacrifice. Red is active and hot, it jumps forward and attracts attention. Long associated with love and romance, it shows passion, but it also signals "stop."

- Use red carefully and sparingly in decorating. It excites and even incites. It is believed to increase the flow of adrenaline, increase our blood pressure, and speed up our heartbeat. It can stimulate the pituitary gland, stimulate our appetite, and even stimulate conversation.

- It encourages action. In its lightest tint, pink, it is calming and has even been used on the walls of correctional institutions to control behavior.

- Men usually prefer yellow-based reds and women prefer cool blue-based reds and pinks.

- Deep cranberry and maroon seem to appeal to an upper socioeconomic group.

- *Idiom: "Paint the town red"*

YELLOW
Cheerful and urgent

- This color makes a rapid first impression and expresses immediacy — it's highly visible and draws attention. It is also known to speed up metabolism.

- It is considered an imperial color symbolizing intellectual and spiritual enlightenment.

- It symbolizes the sun, wealth, warmth and summer.

- Yellow is bright, airy and welcoming. It is a good color for dark or small areas and for warming rooms facing north.

- Although it is cheerful and happy, a bright yellow on four walls can be tiring and cause anxiety. Babies are said to be more anxious in a yellow nursery.

- Bright yellow is less tolerated with age. They say that after age 65, colors may all take on a yellowish cast.

- Gold in a dressing room can make the complexion look sallow.

- Yellow also signals caution along with cowardice.

- *Idiom: "Golden opportunity"*

ORANGE
Warm and communicative

- Orange too is a sunny color that carries much the same associations as red and yellow. It is warming in its entire range, from tints like light peach and shrimp, to deep shades of burnt orange or rust.

- In its light to medium shades, orange makes for a friendly, cheerful atmosphere.

- Muted orange is viewed as informal, a comfortable color for family rooms or gathering areas.

- It can be heavy-looking and annoying in its pure full intensity.

- Use it carefully; it can be overwhelming in large quantities.

- If you are watching your weight, keep away from rooms and eating establishments with warm-colored walls. They tend to stimulate your thirst and appetite. Smile.

- *Idiom: "Glowing orange eyes"*

COOL COLORS
Blue, green, and purple
Cool colors are associated with water and sky and are sometimes called evening colors.

BLUE
Royal and tranquil
- Stands for honor and valor.

- The Egyptians cherished blue, and it has always been symbolic of royalty because it was costly to produce and only a king could afford it. Some eastern cultures associate it with immortality.

- Blue is calming, restful and cool, a good choice to cool down rooms facing the sunny side of the street.

- Blue is the most widely used color for bedrooms, followed by living rooms.

- It is also a popular color for clothing. The darker the shade, the stronger an image of pride is conveyed.

- In a tint, blue ranges from cool to calming to even tranquilizing.

- In a deep shade, such as navy, it represents trustworthiness and stability but can feel rather confining on four walls.

- Some shades of blue-green are not good for small dining areas. They can reflect on the food, causing it to look unappetizing (great if you're watching your weight!).

- Women seem to prefer aqua blues or blue-greens and men the purer hue.

- *Idiom :"Feeling blue"*

GREEN
Natural and soothing

- The color of nature. It represents cool fresh meadows, springtime, hope, and the renewal of life. (Notice green is often the color on recycling products and natural foods).

- On the other hand, envy and fear are also associated with green.

- Green is said to enhance concentration. Maybe that's why TV performers and guests relax in what's called the "green room" before going "on the air." Green is soothing for rooms with a southern exposure. Soft tints are relaxing in a bedroom, work areas, and offices.

- The deeper and richer the color the more prestigious it appears.

- Muted shades are not the most appetizing in eating spaces. An example is avocado green.

- Note that green is considered a transitional color. It is the only color on the color wheel that can be interpreted as warm or cool. It depends on the amount of (warm) yellow or (cool) blue that is mixed with it.

- *Idiom: "Green with envy"*

PURPLE
Powerful and introspective

- The most magical color of all. Purple is a color of power and wisdom, and gives an impression of formality. Like blue, it is associated with royalty. Its "royal" quality originated because it was difficult to produce. The dye came from "the high seas." Only those of wealth could afford to have it, and hundreds of thousands of squids gave up their lives so that the Roman Emperors could wear robes of purple.

- Some cultures and religions associate it with death and mourning.

- It is also associated with the first flowers of spring.

- In muted tones it is favored by upper socio-economic groups.

- *Idiom: "Purple with rage"*

BROWN
Ageless and natural

- Brown is a mixture of red, yellow, and blue in equal amounts.

- It represents the earth and gives a natural,

THE UNCOLORS
Brown
White
Gray
Black

comfortable, secure feeling.

- A soothing and warming color that blends well with any scheme. It is one of the "uncolors" like white, grey and black — not to minimize its importance.

- It can enhance all color schemes and combinations in its various tones or even stand alone with accents of white and black. Textures and patterns give it life.

- Beige is especially popular. It is a safe color for walls and carpeting.

- *Idiom: "Brown as a berry"*

GRAY
Uncommitted and uninvolved

- Gray is one of the neutrals and like browns and beiges, it enhances any color scheme. Gray is a tint of black.

- It is a "classic" color, and always in style.

- It can carry either warm or cool undertones, so select it carefully to blend with your warm or cool palette.

- Gray is said to be non-committal, a good color to use when trying to tone down or quiet a vibrant scheme. Alone, it is a poor choice for retail shops. It's not enough to stimulate sales or excitement.

- It can make a room feel cold without another color.

- *Idiom: "Gray as a battleship"*

BLACK
Classic and moody

- A sophisticated enhancer and a show-off. It contrasts with most colors and thus helps them stand out too.

The deeper the colors, the deeper the neutrals can be; the lighter the colors in a room, the lighter in value the neutrals. A deep charcoal gray makes a smoother transition with light colors than a black would. White is always pleasing for an interesting contrast.

- Alone it can be stark or dreary and depressing.

- In some cultures black is associated with death and mourning.

- Black is a great anchor color for strong palettes and is even good with other neutrals. Grays and beiges, however, are better neutrals for lighter color palettes. Like brown and white, it is ageless and never out of style.

- *Idiom: "It's as clear as black and white"*

WHITE
Fresh and pure

- White projects cleanliness and purity.

- Pure white on large areas can seem harsh and cold. It is best when toned with a warm undertone.

- White is another "palette pleaser," a great color to use in a scheme to show off other colors.

- When used as a contrast, white can be perky and can easily transform a dull room into a crisp-looking one. It is especially effective as a wood trim color.

- White is a color of mourning for the Chinese.

- Know that the "off" in off-white can make or break a room depending on its warm or cool underlying base color. It can make a room feel warm or cold.

- *Idiom: "White as a sheet"*

An entire neutral-colored room is very relaxing, but can also become boring unless you perk it up with a contrast of values and textures.

Now, next time you're out and about, pay attention to your surroundings. You'll know what color is saying to you!

SHOW YOUR COLORS JUST FOR FUN!

Zero-in on the colors you like best. It makes a difference in the way you feel! And don't be surprised if the colors you like to wear are different than those you like to live with.

Who knows why or where our color preferences began or when they will change? Maybe the following fun exercise will reveal how you feel about certain colors. It may help with making decisions for your home. Look at the list of colors below and write down the first thing that comes to your mind in response to each column. See what person, place or thing you link with it, what emotion it triggers and what visual temperature it evokes from you.

Example

Color: Green

A. meadow

B. relaxed

C. cool

A = the person, place, or thing you associate with the color.

B = The emotional feelings the color brings out in you.

C = The physical warm or cool reaction you have to that color.

	A association	**B** feeling	**C** warm or cool
Red			
Pink			
Orange			
Peach			

	A association	B feeling	C warm or cool
Yellow			
Gold			
Green			
Olive Green			
Purple			
Lavender			
Light Blue			
Navy			
White			
Black			
Charcoal			
Brown			
Beige			
Gray			

My favorite color is _____

My least favorite color is _____

YOUR COLORSCOPE

Believe it or not!

Take some time to find out what your color choice reveals about your inner self, or so they say!

"Beauty is in the eye of the beholder." There are colors, tints, shades, intensities and combinations that particularly appeal to each one of us. We simply enjoy one more than another. Our personal color perceptions and preferences begin in childhood and continue and change as we grow and mature. We associate certain colors with certain things, and our likes and dislikes take shape. Many observations have been made on color preferences and personality. Color researchers believe that color choices can be linked to temperament, character, and disposition.

For fun, see what your favorite color says about you. Find out what your "color horoscope" is, some famous people who share your color, and the most compatible color preferences for friends or mates.

Note: Included under each color is the entire range of colors per "color family," from its tints to shades and mixtures and any of their given names. For example, the color red here includes pink, cotton candy, cranberry, burgundy, maroon, and so on. Preferences for darker shades could mean a more intense personality.

RED *a zest for life*

Characteristics

leader
competitive
cheerful
impulsive
expressive
courageous

extrovert
passionate
energetic
athletic
strong-willed

Color Mate
red or orange

Famous People
Abraham Lincoln
Liza Minelli
Carol Burnett
Altovese Davis
Stephanie Mills
Theodore Roosevelt

ORANGE *chitter chatter*

Characteristics

communicative
energetic
assertive
successful
wholesome
quick-witted

gregarious
charming
persuasive
has lots of friends
gourmet cook
can be fickle

Color Mate
orange or red

Famous People
P.T. Barnum
Telly Savalas
Ed Asner
Melissa Gilbert
Andy Williams
Lynn Redgrave

YELLOW *keep your sunny side up*

Characteristics

cheerful
warm
optimistic
intellectual
idealistic
proud
a good friend

strong willed
original
imaginative
artistic
perfectionist
egotistical

Color Mate
purple or yellow

Famous People
Dinah Shore
Confucius
Lola Falana
Erik Estrada
Jane Seymour
Linda Evans

PURPLE *mystery and intrigue*

Characteristics

easy to live with
genius
confident
artistic
individualistic
strong values

unconventional
sophisticated
spiritual
quick perception
sincere
not impulsive

Color Mate yellow best or red, blue, green

Famous People

Louis Pasteur
Edgar Allan Poe
Liz Taylor
Connie Chung
Robert Redford
Barbra Streisand

BLUE *confident yet vulnerable*

Characteristics

conservative
introverted
intellectual
quiet
loyal
enthusiastic
organized
trusting

harmony-minded
patient
persevering
thinks twice
vulnerable
anticipates wealth
boater

Color Mate green or blue

Famous People

Charles Lindbergh
Melissa Manchester
Robert Wagner
Cary Grant
Candice Bergen
Kristy McNichol
George Washington

GREEN *never fear when green is near*

Characteristics

serene
courageous
assertive
dependable
positive
tolerant
understanding

optimistic
naturalist
high moral standards
loyal neighbor
stable
well balanced
likes money

Color Mate red or green

Famous People

Shakespeare
Princess Diana
Cheryl Tiegs
Kris Kristofferson
Prince Charles
Jamie Farr
Oprah Winfrey

BROWN *a friend indeed*

Characteristics

reliable
stable
person of
  substance
sense of humor
devoted to
  home & hearth

good money
  manager
need for security
good companion
good parent
warm
quality-minded

Color Mate
orange or green

Famous People
Paul Newman
Phyllis Diller
Lauren Bacall
Buddy Hackett
Christopher Reeve
Charles Dickens

WHITE *precise and to the point*

Characteristics

youthful
neat home
self-sufficient
critical
fussy
meticulous dresser

budget conscious
firm and precise
perfectionist
spiritual
easy to get along with

Color Mate
yellow or green

Famous People
Carol Channing
John Travolta
Victoria Principal
Steve Martin

How I learned to mix brown

It began quite innocently. I was in kindergarten, and at last it was my turn to paint at the easel. I was so excited! But my memories are bittersweet. As I stepped back to admire my happy smiling sun, it began to run. Its bright yellow rays slowly slid into the blue sky, turning it green, and the red tulips into orange, while my blue sky swam into the remaining red tulips and turned them purple. And it wasn't over yet! My eyes got as big as saucers where it all came to a sudden stop at the bottom of the paper. There they all rested together in a puddle of brown mud. Talk about defying the laws of gravity! To this day, I don't understand how water colors were expected to adhere to a smooth surface on a vertical plane. But after all, I guess it was a good lesson in mixing colors. I learned that red, yellow and blue mixed together make brown.

Thanks to computers and chemical technology, the manufacturers have taken care of mixing the pigments for us. All we have to do is pick and choose the color that's exactly right for the job.

2
THE
TRICKY SIDE
OF COLOR

**Special Effects
Using Color Instead
Of A Hammer**

When building or remodeling, consider which direction you want your kitchen or bedrooms to face for maximum or minimum natural sunlight.

THE TRICKY SIDE OF COLOR
IS IT MAGIC OR ILLUSION?
It's acutally a matter of light!

SPECIAL EFFECTS

Color can create optical illusions by the amount and intensity of light that strikes it. Light is color's accomplice. Color is affected differently by natural and artificial light, and by the color next to it. Color takes you beyond "what goes with what." Light adds another dimension. Together they can cast a mood, alter apparent space and room temperature, and even enhance or camouflage furniture, furnishings and architectural details by contrast. Learning how to master light and color gives you the power to control and create the illusions you want. Here are the illusions. Use them to create magic.

1. ALTER SPACE

LIGHT COLORS reflect light, and thus they visually appear to push out and expand space. DARK COLORS do the opposite because they absorb light. They can turn a large space into a cozy and more dramatic place.

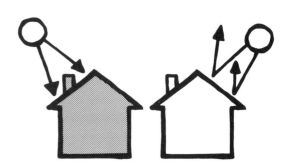

2. MOOD MAKERS

There are colors that can make us "feel" a certain way. Use the colors you love. Surround yourself with colors that make you happy and relaxed. Create an atmosphere to suit you and the activity of the room. What one person deems cheerful may cause another to feel edgy. Generally, we associate certain colors with past experiences. (Review Section 1 for more about how colors can make you feel.)

3. HEAT WAVES OR COLD SPELLS

Sunny or cool — it's up to you. Reds, oranges and yellows dominate one half of the color wheel. These are the warm sun colors. Rooms that face north or east get cool natural light and can be flattered or visually "warmed up" with sunny colors. On the other hand, those that face the sunny south and west sides of the street can be teamed up with a dominance of evening hues: greens, blues, and purples to cool them down.

4. DISAPPEARING ACTS

Before you make any purchase, ask yourself if you want whatever it is to blend or contrast with its sur-roundings. This includes everything inside and out, from hardware to the pictures on the walls.

Contrast and camouflage with color. This applies to everything from paint to fabrics, wood trim and furniture. To enhance a feature such as a fireplace or architectural detail, contrast its color to its background to make it stand out. If it's an unsightly radiator heat duct or an out of place win-dow, camouflage it by painting it the same color of its background. For furniture or anything that seems too large for a small room, you can also diminish its bulk or make it less noticeable by selecting a fabric that's close to the carpeting and/or wall color.

Interesting examples of how color can play tricks on our eyes can be found by studying impressionist paintings. The French Impressionist George Seurat (1859-1891) was one of a group of artists who manipulated color and light to create special effects. His painting "La Grande Jatte"* shows a painstaking technique called "pointillism" that eliminates brush strokes. The painting portrays people enjoying a sunny day on a Paris river bank. He placed minute dots juxtapositioned so that the eye would naturally blend them from a distance. For example, dots of the primary colors set next to each other visually mix and create secondary colors from a distance. It's worth a trip to the museum to take a closer look. When you find one of these types of paintings, step back and see how the colors blend into each other.

*Fully titled: A Sunday Afternoon on La Grande Jatte; oil on canvas, 82 3/4" x 121 1/4." This painting can be found at The Art Institute of Chicago.

HOW TO REMODEL WITH COLOR INSTEAD OF A HAMMER

Use the illusions of color to get more house out of your home

You can change the visual dimensions and feeling of a space in any room by knowing how to manipulate the color and light on walls, ceilings, floors, window coverings, wood furniture, accessories, lighting, and textures. Changing the wall color may have a bigger impact than simply adding a color-coordinated throw pillow. Every change, from biggest to smallest will add up to the total look. The following elements are listed in order of those having the biggest impact of change to those that create the smallest change. Many of these projects can be handled on a weekend.

A. REMODELING WALLS
REMODELING WALLS WITH PAINT

- With the swish of a brush, you can hide unsightly architectural features; erase steam radiators, heat ducts, pipes and air conditioning units; and play down out of place built-ins and "not-so-attractive" woodwork or window frames.

- Paint is by far the quickest and most cost-effective way to alter space. You get the most mileage out of a gallon of paint for your money. The average person can easily achieve near-professional results in no time. Ask your paint dealer about the many new techniques to achieve special effects with sponge painting or rag rolling.

- For unity in small homes and rooms that open into each other, let the wall color, wood trim, or floor covering color flow from room to

If your teenager wants to paint the bedroom walls black, don't panic — he or she is just expressing a sense of individuality. However, when it's time to cover the black, hand over the paint brush!

Don't panic!
Give paint a
chance to dry.
Light colors dry
darker and dark
colors dry
lighter.

room. Treat them as a unit. Since bedrooms are usually in another area of the house separated by a door, it's okay to paint them a different color. Hallways and stairwells should remain neutral. They make a smooth color transition to rooms that open into them.

- To enhance a feature, merely paint it a little deeper, or contrast it to its background, and make it a focal point of the room.

- Use paint inside or out to transform walls, ceilings, woodwork trim, doors, and floors. Since walls are the largest areas in our homes, they are the surest and quickest way to change the entire look of a room. This is also the most effective way to instantly refresh it. To visually increase the size of an area, paint the walls a light color. Even if you do nothing else, a light tint of any color will do a lot to "enlarge" any room.

TYPES OF PAINT FINISHES

Select your paint by durability and finish, along with color. Bear in mind that each of the following reflect light differently. The less reflective the finish, the better to hide uneven walls.

PAINT FINISHES

Flat paint — looks like suede, does not reflect light and does not clean as well as other finishes. Use on ceilings. It has a chalky appearance.

Eggshell — has a slight sheen. It can be used on walls and wood trim, and is good for bedrooms and living rooms.

Satin — has a litte more sheen and is good for wood trim.

Semi-gloss — Is more reflective than eggshell and satin. Very good for wood trim and rooms that need to be very washable, such as kitchens and bathrooms.

High gloss — is highly reflective and very durable, but shows every imperfection. Use carefully!

REMODELING WALLS WITH WALLPAPER

- Wallpaper can alter as well as decorate space by the same rules of color that we've used for paint. Do you need to visually increase space? If so, look for an open-pattern wallpaper with a light-colored background and soft contrasting colors with small designs or motifs. Papers with light backgrounds increase space, especially in patterns such as lattice or windowpane. Dark patterns do the opposite, bringing the walls in and cozying things up.

- The patterns and design of wallpaper can also alter the visual height and width of a room. Vertical lines and stripes can lift a ceiling, a horizontal pattern can lower the look of a tall room, and a diagonal line or motif can give it movement or perspective.

- To lower a high ceiling, you can also use a wallpaper border at the top of the walls. Match the scale of the pattern to the size of the room.

- Large rooms can carry larger patterns, and vice versa. Use wallpaper with small patterns and texture in small rooms or those interrupted by lots of cabinets, doors, appliances, or windows. A large pattern would lose its continuity and look too cut up. Be careful of plaids or stripes if your walls are not plumb.

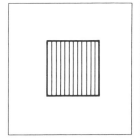

VERTICAL DESIGN

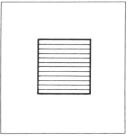

HORIZONTAL DESIGN

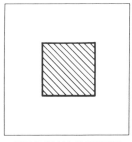

DIAGONAL DESIGN

43

REMODELING WALLS WITH PANELING

- When you're trying to decide on a wood color finish for paneling, apply the same rules of dark colors shrinking, and light colors expanding space.

- Stain is trickier than paint. Not only must you consider the warm or cool tone of the stain, but also the inherent color of the species of the wood. Each variety of wood has its own natural color, and absorbs differently depending on the hardness or softness of the wood fibers. Raw wood is like a sponge.

- Too shiny a finish on paneling can actually make a space seem smaller because it draws attention by the light it reflects.

- Test a few stain colors on sample pieces to make sure you're getting the exact tone you're after.

- Most paneling, including that which is only simulated wood, has thin vertical seams between the "boards." Vertical lines have the effect of lifting the eye and raising the

---

SPECIES OF WOOD:
HARDNESS, GRAIN AND NATURAL COLOR

OAK
Hardwood
Bold grain
Light grayish
Brown to reddish
  brown

CEDAR
Hardwood
Even grain
Repels moths
Reddish color

CHERRY
Hardwood
Fine, even grain
Pale yellow to
  reddish brown

MAPLE
Hardwood
Even grain
Creamy white to
  reddish brown

PINE
Softwood/very
  absorbant
Uneven grain
Yellow white to
  reddish brown

ceiling a bit. Here, too, you'll want to follow the rule of room proportion when it comes to deciding on wide versus narrow panels. The smaller a room, the narrower they should be.

B. REMODELING THE CEILING

- The ceiling color also affects the visual space of a room. You can "raise" it by painting it lighter than the walls, especially a white tone. This gives it a reflective quality that will carry your eye up and "lift" the ceiling. Pictures with vertical dimensions can "lift" the ceiling, as well as wallpaper with vertical stripes.

- To pull down a high ceiling, paint it a little deeper color than the walls, or even consider covering it with a wallpaper that coordinates with the room.

- Wallpaper borders at the ceiling or at chair rail height can cut a high ceiling. A horizontal patterned wallpaper can do the same. Horizontal picture arrangements diminish the height of a room, as do chair rails (the average height is 36" from the floor).

- To give a flat ceiling a coved look, install a piece of wood trim 1" to 2" wide on all four walls, 4" to 6" from the ceiling. Paint from the wood trim to the top of the wall and continue onto the ceiling, all with the same color. Apply paper below the trim, or paint of a different color.

CEILING TILE

- A key factor here is keeping the size of the squares in proportion to the size of the room. As for texture in ceiling tiles, a smoother texture will give a lighter and airier affect in a standard height room. A heavy texture will weigh it down.

- If you want to draw less attention to the height of a dropped ceiling, keep cross bars or braces the same color as the squares. Contrasting braces visually bring the ceiling down.

C. REMODELING THE FLOOR

- Don't overlook the floor. Think of it as the "fifth wall" of a room. After all, it's the next largest area of color in a room.

- You can increase visual space by selecting a floor covering the same color as your walls, or just a touch deeper or lighter.

- Large patterns and deep shades in carpeting tend to visually decrease the floor space of a room.

- Wall-to-wall carpeting will increase space as compared to an area rug, which cuts the space, especially if it contrasts with the floor beneath it. However, an area rug close to the floor color, gives the same effect of wall to wall carpeting.

- To give a room a floating feeling, make the ceiling and floor match in a light color and the walls a deeper color.

- Wall-to-wall carpet or area rugs with a contrasting color border can visually scale down floor space.

Keep floor materials and designs in proportion to the floor space — small for small areas, and vice versa.

- Stay away from borders unless your room is at least 12' x 16'. For a more spacious feeling and a smoother flow from room to room, use the same color carpeting in rooms that open into each other.

- Wood floors also have color stains or washes. Apply the same rules of dark colors shrinking, and lighter colors expanding space. For an interesting and expanding illusion,

46

install floor boards on the diagonal. This effect can also be achieved by doing the same with tile, bricks, marble squares, and so on. See sketch below.

• Don't paint baseboards a contrasting color to your walls or carpet; it will only chop up your room. Rather, paint them to blend with your walls. A neutral such as off-white is always acceptable, even if the floors and walls are the same color.

• Vinyl flooring comes in many finishes, textures and patterns as well as colors. For less work, avoid light, one color or smooth surfaces. They could end up being dirt traps, especially in high traffic areas used by children or pets. Also consider the durability and maintenance of the product.

Wood floors, tile, marble, brick, etc. installed on the diagonal visually expands space. Compare the boxes.

D. REMODELING THE WINDOWS

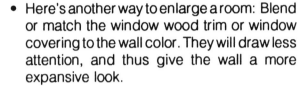

- Here's another way to enlarge a room: Blend or match the window wood trim or window covering to the wall color. They will draw less attention, and thus give the wall a more expansive look.

- For attention or a cozier look, use a fabric or shade that contrasts with the walls, thus cutting the expanse of the wall.

- A wallpaper border around a small window will not only dress it up but also enlarge it. This is an inexpensive way to give a window a "curtained," warmer look.

A rule of thumb for valance lengths: Measure from the top of where the valance is to hang, down to the floor. Now divide that number by 6 for the correct valance length.

Example:

84" = (top of valance to floor)

84" ÷ 6 = 14" valance

- To hide uneven or out of place windows, paint the trim the same color as the walls and/or use a window covering that matches the wall color.

- To widen, center, or balance a window on the wall, adjust the side panels of curtains or drapes to extend beyond each side accordingly, covering more window on one side and more wall on the other until they look even.

- To decrease the size of a window, do not extend the window covering beyond the wood trim — rather cover only the window.

- To lengthen a window, simply install a valance at the ceiling instead of at the top of the window. Drapes or curtains that go to the floor make a window look taller.

E. REMODELING THE FURNITURE

- Wood furniture that blends with the color of the walls and carpeting seems to melt into it. This is a great way to diminish the size of a piece of furniture that seems too large for the room.

- To draw attention to a certain piece or accent, on the other hand, contrast it to its surroundings.

- Upholstered furniture, likewise, can be camouflaged by painting the wall the background color of the fabric. To spotlight it, do the opposite. Paint the wall one of the least dominant colors in the fabric.

- Pattern makes a difference, too. Keep the size of the motif in proportion to the piece — large patterns on larger pieces and vice versa.

F. REMODELING WITH ACCESSORIES

- Accessories are the smallest areas of change, but that doesn't mean you shouldn't take great care in selecting them — especially for a small room. A lot of different-colored stuff scattered here and there fights for attention, and can give the "color jitters." To solve this, repeat one accessory color in at least three other places in the room to carry your eye smoothly across.

- Accessories, like any other element in a room, can either blend or contrast with their surroundings. Light-colored things, of course, reflect more light and look larger, especially against a dark background.

- To minimize an overly prominent dark accent piece, place it against a background of the same color. If, on the other hand, it is something — say, a large vase on a pedestal — which is meant to be focal point, highlight it with an overhead spotlight.

G. REMODELING WITH LIGHTING

- A room can be made to seem more spacious just by putting a table lamp in a corner, where it will light up two walls at once.

- Backlighting furniture will create expansive visual space. Up-lights or canister spots on the floor behind furniture, for example, cast shadows and create the illusion of open space.

- Lights over pictures, behind furniture, in corners, and dimmers create a cozy feeling.

- Try a tinted bulb to enhance the color in a room. Rose is a popular color.

- Different types of lampshades can also change the appearance of color. Dark opaques absorb more light and some colors even cast their color into the room.

- Bear in mind that low wattage bulbs have a tendency to make colors look drab.

- Darker rooms absorb more light, you may need more wattage.

H. REMODELING WITH TEXTURE

- The heavier the texture on a wall, fabric, or piece of furniture, the more light it will absorb and the heavier it will look. The surface of anything, no matter what color, will absorb more light if it is a matte finish (non-shiny) as compared to a shiny one.

- Shiny finishes make colors seem more vivid because they reflect more light.

- Texture gives warmth to a room. Use only two or three different textures per room. Extreme textures in a room, such as silk with brick, are too different and create discord.

- Rough textures on walls, furniture, and floors contribute to a casual look.

- Grass cloth or heavily textured wallpapers camouflage uneven walls.

- Smooth surfaces visually expand and give a more formal feeling.

- If you'd like to create texture for warmth where there is none, consider creating the illusion with various paint techniques, called faux finishes.

Faux is a French word that means "false." Techniques to create visual texture such as sponge painting and rag rolling are popular and simple to do. They can do a nice job to camouflage uneven walls. "Trompe d'oeil" (another French term, meaning "to deceive the eye") is creating something that really isn't there, such as painting a fake window or a door, a scenic wall, or an area rug painted on a wood floor. Be careful before you embark on any of these more complicated projects — they'll require a little more skill than faux painting.

A CHECKLIST BEFORE YOU SHOP

To avoid costly color mistakes

Never shop for groceries on an empty stomach — or home products when you are starved for color. Avoid hasty or useless sale item decisions. Always be ready with your color plan.

☑ **Only select your colors in the rooms** they will occupy, in the natural daylight and/or in the artificial, evening lighting. If the room is used mostly in the evening, select your colors at that time. If the room is used throughout the day, study your colors during that time.

☑ **Bring home "king" size samples** for an accurate light reading. Remember, color becomes more intense with quantity. Bring all samples together and observe how they look with each other. If it's shingles, throw them on the roof. NOTE: For an accurate reading, it's best to select exterior colors on a cloudy day, rather than a bright, sunny day.

Always consider your light source.

Try samples on: Tape wallpaper to the wall, set carpeting samples under the leg of a chair, drape fabric over the furniture and paint a 2' x 2' poster board the color you are considering for your walls. Examine it against all four walls, because lighting will make it look different on each. Be sure you like them all.

Stick to your color plan (which is what you'll be creating next). Don't buy on impulse. Always record complete information of every product: the manufacturer, the code numbers and especially the dye lots. When it comes to carpeting, fabrics and wallpaper, there can be mix-ups, so hang on to your samples and numbers and compare them.

A word about trends: They can become old overnight. Unless you can afford to change every couple of years, invest in colors you love and can live with, especially your fixed or big ticket items. However, you can inject trendy things into your home in less costly accents, such as lampshades, throw pillows, place mats and napkins, floral arrangements, etc. The rule here is to repeat a color in at least three other places in the room for balance. You can use different values.

3
COLORS THAT SAY HOME TO YOU

How To Give It Your Personal Stamp

DRESS YOUR HOME TO SUIT YOUR TASTE

HOMESTYLE TIPS

- The fun part of decorating is adding a little style or theme to your rooms. The trend today is to tailor your spaces to represent your individuality. Following a style or theme simplifies making color and decorating decisions.

- Think in terms of a *theme* to go along with the color and style of your furniture. You can get ideas from vacation pictures, postcards — even your dreams. Just picture it! Turn your dining room into a California vineyard, your kitchen into a French café, a dark musty basement into a tropical island, or a child's room into a "three-ring circus." Be creative — update that beautiful knotty pine attic, den or basement and turn it into a cabin in the north woods. Unlock your imagination ... go for it! Turn dull, unforgiving spaces into exciting new places.

- Retailers are geared to grouping fabric samples, wallpapers and furniture by style. This also holds true for light fixtures, cabinets, hardware, wood moldings and so on. In fact, most products are sold by *style and color*.

- We seem to associate our feelings for style and color with places that have made an impression on us. It could have been many years ago visiting with grandma, or more recently at a neighbor's home, or even a furniture showroom.

- Basically there are two categories of home styles: one linked to the past and the other modern.

Whether you do-it-yourself or are working with a professional, pick a style that suits you.

5 *Where do you fit in?*
MOST COMMON STYLES:

1. CONTEMPORARY

Contemporary homes seem to attract chic and artistic people. They love the purity of line and form from furnishings to architecture. They love nature and the arts, and may even "dabble" in painting, sculpture or photography. These works are beautifully and proudly displayed throughout the home. Entertaining at home is most enjoyable. This style is open and easy to maintain.

2. COUNTRY

You'll find a country home-style type of person relaxing at the kitchen table with family and friends. A sense of quality of life, nature and the finest craftsmanship often define the characteristics of those who love country. These folks spend holidays and weekends searching for yet another antique or special item. Good furniture reproductions and handmade items adorn their homes. Some of the lovely sights, sounds and smells you'll find woven throughout this kind of home could range from soft music and fine French cuisine, to home-canned peaches and cakes made from scratch.

3. VICTORIAN

Victorian homes are for romantics and those that appreciate the painstaking work that went into every piece of wood, glass and marble. These homes cast a spell of yesteryear. Lots of things everywhere creates a strong atmosphere that embraces you the moment you enter the home. It can whisk you away from the bustle of the city to a delightful sense of peace. Warm and charming personalities grace this home.

4. TRADITIONAL

You won't find trendy things here. Strong-willed and determined, this personality is somewhat of a perfectionist, yet fun-loving as well as serious. Those who prefer this style will look for detail, fine craftsmanship, *and* the comfort of grandma's furniture. Rich woods and colors are a feast for their eyes. They too are always searching for authentic pieces of furniture such as Hepplewhite, Chippendale or Adams (styles named after the persons that originally hand-crafted the items), but will settle for good reproductions.

5. ECLECTIC (E'KLEK-TIK, adj.)

Eclectic homes are for people of many interests who enjoy all of the above. They are likely to go browsing for antiques on weekends and stop at every contemporary studio along the way. "Dabblers" too, they wish they had more time to pursue a class in making leaded glass windows. Family and friends are not surprised to find an antique chair covered with a contemporary fabric or something new or different each time they visit.

A BRIGHT IDEA!

JUST PICTURE IT!

Here's a little trick to help you try on some new colors for your home inside or out before you begin shopping.

1. Photograph the area.

1. Take a picture of your project, room or exterior. In fact while you're at it, photograph your entire home. It's a good record for insurance purposes as well as before and after projects.

2. Enlarge it on a copier.

2. Process the film and enlarge the photos on a copy machine. For extra large copies, keep enlarging the copy.

3. Outline the room and furniture with a black marker on white paper.

3. Now tape the black and white copy to a window and place a sheet of paper over it. Outline the entire area and everything in it with a thin line black marker. Details are not important, it's the shapes you want to capture. Now color in the areas with crayons or colored pencils for an idea of how the new colors blend and where you want them.

4. Color it in!

4. Tuck your enlargements into a file folder with the original photo for future reference.

COLORS THAT SAY HOME TO YOU

Add your personal stamp

Consider color-fastness for rooms that get direct sunlight.

Many styles and colors have historical and cultural links. However, don't feel you are restricted to any of them. Colors that were popular in yesteryears were limited by the availability of chemicals and dyes and the knowledge to mass produce them. It was not until the mid-nineteenth century that technology exploded with color.

Select colors that "feel" right; after all, this is *your home — express yourself!* Here's a quick reference to get you thinking. This is by no means a complete list, just the highlights of a few styles. Then visit a furniture showroom for a full visual panorama.

ARE YOU CONTEMPORARY?

Smooth, linear designs are the beauty and focal points of this style. Lots of windows bring in nature and streams of light.

The Mood
Spaciousness and uncluttered rooms that open up into each other.

Furniture
Simple, straight lines on upholstered pieces, and a mixture of light woods, lucite, brass, metal and glass for accessories and accents.

Colors
Usually monochromatic. One color or neutrals with strong accents such as black, red or yellow.

Patterns and Textures
Natural materials, such as brick, stone, and tile. Wood floors, area rugs or low-pile wall to wall carpeting. Textured or smooth walls. Window coverings are optional. Patterns are usually plaids, stripes and various motifs depending on a particular theme.

Accents
Colorful paintings, sculpture, mirrors and "artsy" stuff. Fresh flowers in crystal clear containers, track lighting and floor lamps.

ARE YOU A LITTLE BIT COUNTRY? _____

The Mood
"Home sweet home." A touch of yesteryear. Simplicity and romance. Warm, cozy, casual and relaxed. A put-your-feet-up kind of place.

Furniture
Comfortable, overstuffed pieces, to rocking chairs and foot stools. Curved lines and strong, sturdy functional tables and lamps. Representations of functional tools such as a "butterchurn" lamp base, might grace an end table. Twig chairs and log furniture.

Colors
"Grayed down" or dusty neutrals to vivid blues, reds, rust, yellow, green and warm whites.

Textures and patterns
Brick and stone, natural warm woods, painted or stained trim and floors, and braided rag rugs. Checkered window coverings, denim, gingham and plaid patterns or floral and natural motifs taken from nature or the barn yard. Rough-sawn beams. Log or paneled walls to check or stripe wallpaper.

Accents

Collectibles, handmade anything, handicrafts, dried floral arrangements, quilts hanging or draped over furniture, afghans, pewter and tinware, wicker and stenciled walls and borders. Primitive family portraits, paintings and working tools for decoration.

ARE YOU A VICTORIAN ROMANTIC? ___

The Mood

Elegant and formal, yet warm and cozy. The atmosphere is busy and heavy with dark colors and could be depressing for some, save for all the "bric-brac" (knick-knacks). High ceilings and large rooms with double doors and wide trim embrace you with their warm, natural wood tones and detail.

Furniture

Carved wood and lots of curved lines. Most upholstered pieces are heavily adorned with wood trim. Wood tables and fern stands are topped with marble. The most simple fireplace exudes elegance. You might even find petticoat mirrors built into the bottom of buffets or sideboards to check that your petticoat isn't showing!

Colors

Deep rich colors on walls, woodwork and furnishings, and jewel toned stained glass windows.

Textures and patterns

You guessed it! Tone on tone richly patterned fabrics from velvet, silks and satins to needlepoint on oversized bold scaled furniture. Elaborate doorway and window draperies shade the room with swag upon swag, tassels and fringe.

Accents

Hand-painted lamp globes, to elegant crystal chandeliers, wall sconces and medallions on the ceiling. Family portraits, hand-woven "hair" pictures under bubble glass frames and melancholy scenes adorn the walls. Stained and etched glass window designs and elegantly carved mirrors, the more the better. Ferns and dried flowers are everywhere. Be sure you love housework for this one!

ARE YOU TRADITIONAL?

The Mood

A stable kind of formal and gracious atmosphere. Timeless! Lots of "nooks and crannies" and beautiful wood trims, painted or stained. Furnishings are inspired by classic designs of the past, Greek, French, Italian, etc.

Furniture

A mixture of straight and curvy line pieces, skirted and exposed chair and sofa legs. Antiques, glazed pieces and a variety of small nests of tables. Average-size furniture, leather chairs and foot stools reflect comfort.

Texture and patterns

Wood paneling, highly-polished warm toned wood floors and woodwork. Wood or fabric covered cornices and decorative drapery rods, swags, Austrian shades and sheer curtains. Polished chintz or cotton fabrics to heavier woven patterns. A mixture of floral patterns with plaids, stripes and sophisticated motifs unified by a key color. Plush wall to wall carpeting and oriental patterned area rugs.

Colors

Rich deep jewel tones, emerald greens, gold, ruby reds and rich blues accented with warm off-whites and some pastels.

Accents

Elegant mirrors, old master paintings with lights over them, framed botanical prints, historical documents and hunting scenes. Porcelain vases and plates on walls or on stands, jade and glass or brass pieces of sculpture and beautiful Persian rugs. Oversized silk, dried and fresh flowers arrangements and topiary trees adorn corners, table tops and entrances.

ECLECTIC (E'KLEK-TIK, adj.)

This style is made up of what seems to be the best of every style — perhaps hundreds of years apart! This is my favorite. It makes a definite personal statement, but be careful, it can be somewhat tricky. Color — not style — is the key that ties it together.

The Mood

Fun, comfortable, relaxing, interesting and ever changing.

Furniture

A collection of personal "treasures and stuff" you love, picked up, collected or inherited over the years. A little bit of all the things you love.

Textures and patterns

A collection of this sort will have many textures and patterns. The bond between them will be a dominant color. Even though this can be the most fun and inexpensive style, to pull it together you may have to reupholster or paint some things. See section 5 on how to mix and match patterns.

Colors

The largest areas of a room are the walls and floors. Blend them using the same color in different values to cradle the "stuff," then focus on two other colors in lesser amounts and repeat them throughout the rooms.

Each room in our home is a different style or theme. The main colors are warm whites, deep rose to cranberry, blue to gray-blues and grey. The unifying color throughout is rose. The complementing accents include a rich blue-green seafoam with deep gray and white neutrals. The floor coverings from room to room range from light bleached wood to tile topped with area rugs, and wall to wall carpeting. Textures, fabrics and patterns include diagonal stripes, florals and polka dots, in cotton to corduroy. The style of the living room is traditional, the kitchen is country, and the bath has a Victorian flavor with lacy shower curtains and baskets of ferns. One bedroom is country French with painted woodwork, and another is contemporary, with a diagonal-patterned wallpaper.

My favorite tropical southwest get-away is my sunporch, with a combination of pastel fabrics, creme and natural wicker furniture upholstered in a stripe, and lots of plants that always seem to need watering! Whatever our mood, we have a room for it! The best part is that most of the furniture is interchangeable from room to room.

So have fun. Live in and love your home! Whether your style is casual or formal, it's how colors flow from room to room that matters.

Dress your home for the season, or just for a change. Store heavy dark stuff for the winter. Bring out the fresh flowers and fun summer colored accents.

BUILD AN IDEA FILE

- Start to build a color and idea file. Collect your ideas and put them in a shoe box. Look through magazines, furniture brochures and catalogs and pull out pictures of things that appeal to you. After a while you will begin to see a color pattern and style emerge that suits your lifestyle.

- Visit furniture showrooms and jot down the color combinations of the displays you like. "A picture is worth a thousand words," so take your camera along and snap a picture. Be aware that the rooms on display are just that. Some of the colors may be too light for comfortable living, especially with active children and playful pets.

- Visit well-decorated model homes, condos, and apartments. They are another good source of inspiration. Again, be aware of the practicality of colors when it comes to maintenance. These rooms are only for show.

WHAT GOES WITH WHAT AND HOW

A. Inside Color Plans
B. Outside Color Plans
C. Brand New
   Home Plans

WHAT COLOR GOES WITH WHAT

Beautiful homes are no accident.
Planning is the key and
color is the most magic element.

A. HOW TO MAKE AN INTERIOR COLOR PLAN

A color plan is just as important to you as a blueprint or building plans are to a builder. It gives you direction. You can create a color plan by selecting colors directly from the color wheel or adapting colors from a ready-made item.

YOUR COLORING TOOLS

The Color Wheel

Paint Color Chips

Let your
favorite colors
take the lead in
organizing your
color plan.

These are the two most important tools in your tool box for making color work.

The **Color Wheel** is really just nature's rainbow twirled into a circle and divided into groups of colors. It shows the relationship of one color to another, those that blend and those that contrast.

The color wheel on the back cover is numbered for easy reference. The outer circle represents the tints of the colors in the center circle. The inner circle represents the shades of the center circle colors.

Half of the color wheel represents warm sun colors and the other half cool evening colors.

The color wheel begins with three primary colors from which all color combinations begin and go on and on.

The primary colors are:

red (#4)

yellow (#12)

blue (#8)

The secondary colors are equal mixtures of the three primaries:

Red + yellow = orange (# 2)

Yellow + blue = green (#10)

Blue + red = purple (#6)

A mixture of a primary with a secondary creates a third color called a tertiary color. Examples of these are numbers 1, 3, 5, 7, 9, 11.

HOW TO CREATE A COLOR PLAN BY JUST USING THE COLOR WHEEL

The color wheel can help you select a brand new scheme or blend new colors into an existing scheme. Think of the color wheel as a large pie cut into 12 wedges and you'll have an easy time of selecting a scheme. Those wedges that are the closest to each other on the wheel create the most harmonious schemes. Those that are the farthest away from each other create a more active scheme. The three most common schemes follow.

Take any one slice out of the pie for a **monochromatic** scheme. This is a one-

neighboring
scheme

contrasting
scheme

Paint displays
have different
types of
lighting above
them. This is to
help you "see"
the colors in
different lights.
However, home
is the only
place you'll get
a true color
reading for
your room.
Remember,
too, that paint
color chips can
vary one to
another. They
change with
age and
exposure to
heat and light.
Select
carefully.

color scheme that can include as many of its tints and shades as you wish. It is easy to do, the most relaxing and the best for expanding space — especially when using light colors. One example of this scheme is wedge #2, or any one other wedge by itself.

Pick any two or three wedges either side of a color and you have a **neighboring** scheme. An example would be wedges 5, 6, and 7. This scheme is more colorful and active-looking.

For drama and contrast, select wedges directly across from each other. This is known as a **complementary,** or **contrasting** scheme. It contains both warm and cool colors. It has an outgoing personality. An example would be wedge #2 with #8, or even #2 with #8 and #9.

PAINT CHIPS AND HOW TO USE THEM

Paint color chips are an extension of each wedge of the color wheel. They are strips of paint color samples found in various values: tints (light) to shades (dark), and intensities from bright to dull. Certainly you've noticed these paint color displays wherever paint is sold. Each manufacturers' display may be set up differently. Some paint strips are arranged like a ladder by values going from light to dark. Others include neighboring colors. Ask your salesperson if you need help.

Select a number of chips representing the values of the color for the type of scheme you've selected and follow steps 1, 3 and 4.

FOUR TURN-KEY STEPS

Read through these steps first, and then refer to Section 6, Your Coloring Workbook. *A sheet has been provided for each step and each room.*

Materials you'll need:

- 1/4" graph paper (or use the paper provided in the Workbook section of this book)
- pencils with erasers
- 12" ruler
- metal or folding tape measure
- scissors
- legal size file folder to glue in samples and swatches or use the pages in Section 6.
- index cards for furniture templates
- shoe box to collect ideas for colors and furniture styles
- typing paper and/or tracing paper for furniture arranging and color sampling
- colored markers, crayons or pencils
- masking tape
- black thin line marker
- glue stick or rubber cement

Optional Materials:
- camera (see "Just Picture It" on page 59)

STEP 1 _____
SIZING UP YOUR SPACE

If you don't have a floor plan of your room , clear off your kitchen table and turn it into a drafting board. Measure your room carefully and transfer it to graph paper using a 1/4" scale to represent one foot. Although this takes a little time, it's well worth it in the long run. Include the height, depth and width of all built-ins such as

Blueprint Symbols

walls

windows

doors

overhead lights

built-ins

electrical outlets

heat ducts

kitchen cabinets and appliances, windows, closets, heat ducts, electrical outlets, swinging and pocket doors. Details . . . details. This will become your most valuable source of information when you begin shopping or ordering materials.

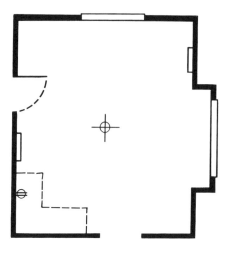

STEP 2
HUNTING FOR A READY-MADE COLOR GUIDE

"What color goes with what?" Now you can have your own personal designer in a snap. It's as easy as using the "shirt on your back." Here's how to do it. Find something with the colors you love. It can be a scarf, dress, tie, shirt, wallpaper, a painting, poster or piece of fabric. Use it for a fool-proof color palette. A designer has already combined what goes with what. All you have to do is distribute the colors into the different spaces on walls, floor, windows, furniture coverings and accessories.

A  BRIGHT IDEA!

WHERE TO HUNT FOR READY-MADE COLOR GUIDES

- Start by looking at your own home with a "curious eye." A place mat or a quilt, a design on a vase, even a throw pillow can become your guide.

- Look in your linen or clothes closet. It's probably filled with colors you like, both solids and prints. However, don't be surprised if some of the colors you wear are not what you'd like on your walls. What flatters you, may not flatter your room!

- Scan a fabric shop. It's filled with great designs in all colors. If you find one you like, purchase a small amount and ask them to hold the rest in case you decide to use it for drapery or furniture coverings. Always identify whatever you purchase by writing down the names and numbers of the piece — especially the dye lot.

- Visit an art gallery or museum. They're filled with lots of inspiring colors you can adapt. A print of a famous masterpiece or poster may end up hanging on your wall, in addition to serving as your color guide.

- Look closely at wallpaper books and window covering catalogs. These often have pictures of well-coordinated rooms.

- If you are still stumped and haven't found a pre-existing guide, seek out a certified interior designer from a design center. A couple of hours of consultation is well worth it.

Before you go on to Step 3, think about a style and/or theme for your room. Dig into your idea file (p. 66).

If you like a particular design but not the colors, ask to see a different "color way" — that means the same design in different colors.

STEP 3 _____
MATCH THE COLORS OF YOUR READY-MADE ITEM TO PAINT CHIPS

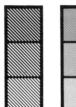

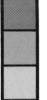

Now that you have an idea of room size, you can begin to put your color plan together. It's time to match up the colors in your ready-made color scheme with paint chip samples. If you are working around an existing fabric or color in the room, let it become your color guide.

Though you may find this process somewhat time-consuming, it is the most accurate approach. Even the most renowned designers use color samples for reference.

Don't panic. Color matches are difficult. They will be a little different because each surface reflects light differently. Remember, for accurate color matches, always take a close look at the color chips in natural light.

A. Take your item to a place that sells paint and pick up some paint chips. Carefully look at the colors in your item and match those colors to the paint chips on display. Also pick out a couple of neutrals: off-whites, grays or browns, and if you are thinking of staining wood trim or floors, pick up stain samples too. Take two samples of each color.

B. Take the paint color strips home and study them in your own lighting. Now you are ready to decide which color goes where, using this formula: Make one color dominate three-quarters of the room, and select two others to use in lesser quantity, plus two neutrals.

74

Two ready-made color schemes

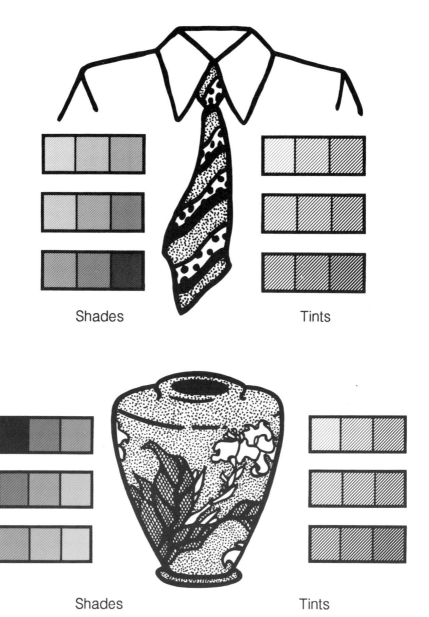

Shades

Tints

Shades

Tints

Here are two sample items that have been matched with color chips. The shades are on the left and the tints on the right.

SAMPLE # COLOR CHIP CHART SAMPLE

(Use this sample chart to follow the steps listed on page 77. Use the pages in Section 6, Your Coloring Work Book, *to plot colors for your home, room by room.)*

1. Wall color   2. Ceiling   3. Wood trim

4. Floor color

5. Fabric colors

6. Accents

7. Neutrals

C. Select and glue a color chip from the ready-made scheme into each of the following areas. Use the pages in Section 6 for a room-by-room plan.

1. The **walls** are the largest area of color that make up the background of your room. Their color usually becomes your key or dominant color. Select a tint to increase the visual space, or go with a deeper shade for drama and coziness.

2. The **ceiling,** like the floor, is a large area. The lighter it is, the more light it reflects, and the higher it seems. It can be an off-white or lighter than the walls.

3. **Wood trim** can be stained, painted, or remain natural. If your main color is warm, select an off-white that contains a warm undertone and vice versa.

4. The **floor** is the next area. Make carpeting the same color as the walls, but a little deeper or lighter. Follow this rule for the key color in an area rug. Use a wood stain sample for wooden floors.

5. Select colors for the **fabrics** next. Take them from the next darkest color in your item. They can be one color or all of the colors in the design. Your window covering color can blend or contrast with the walls depending on whether you want the window coverings to stand out.

6. The deepest colors can be represented in the **accents,** accessories, and small pieces of furniture.

7. Include at least a couple of **neutrals** in your color plan. Stained woods are considered a color, too.

OFF-WHITE: has it ever been OFF? Have you ever had the experience of white looking dirty next to another white? The reason is that the underlying base color may be different. One may be a warm tone and the other a cool tone. You also need to be aware that all neutrals have underlying tones. Avoid mistakes by examining *large samples together in the same light* no matter what they are: carpeting, appliances, paint, siding, and so on.

STEP 4
SHOPPING FOR ACTUAL MATERIALS AND PRODUCTS

Using your color chip chart as a matching guide, you can begin to pull together the actual samples of fabrics, floor, wall and window coverings. Take this book shopping!

Ask for and borrow king-sized samples of each element that matches your chips. Take them home and study the collection of things together in your own light. Live with them for a couple of days before you make any final decisions.

Once you make a final decision, record all information and glue actual samples into your file (designers call this a storyboard). You can use a large poster board instead of a file for a bigger storyboard. You can also use the space provided in the back of this book.

MORE TRICKS OF THE TRADE:

1. **Add some patterns and different textures** in each room for interest and warmth.

2. **When using several patterns** in a room, remember to use them in unequal amounts. Also work in opposite sizes and patterns but keep them in proportion to the scale of the furniture. Most importantly, be sure they all *contain a common color* for unity. Use plaids with stripes, stripes with polka-dots and florals with stripes.

3. **It's a good idea to record all names,** numbers and dye lots on your file for future reference. Like a giant house puzzle, a color plan will assure you that every piece will eventually fit together to complete the picture.

4. **Consider the underlying tone of off-whites.** What is the "off" anyway? It can be a drop of either a warm or cool color. If your dominant room colors are warm then select an off-white with a warm tone and vice versa. When two different undertones meet in the same room, one will make the other look dirty. Also remember that walls reflect off each other, making the color seem more intense. Opt for a tint lighter.

5. **Stained wood trim and floors always look richer** when the walls are not an extreme contrast. A deep cream or beige, rather than white, enhances the wood grain. Painted wood trim should also be a little deeper than the walls. A contrasting color on the crown molding at the ceiling or on chair rails is okay. Just remember what contrast does. It brings the ceiling to attention.

6. **Muted or dusty grayed-down colored walls** look best with muted neutral accents whether it be wood trim or any other element. Be consistent.

7. **Give your furniture some breathing space.** Always place furniture at least 3 to 6 inches away from the walls. It actually makes a room look larger — it's an optical illusion. Try it, you'll be surprised.

Sometimes standing at a distance or squinting at samples together will help you decipher a difference. Our eyes seem to mix colors from a distance. One color next to another can influence its overall look. Always stand back and take another look.

FOUR STEPS
REVIEW

A. What **area** or room are you working on? Do you have the floor plan ready?

B. Have you decided on a scheme for the room? Do you want to enhance the area or furniture by contrast or play them down by **blending** or camouflage?

C. Have you **collected** enough samples and information to know what colors and style or theme you'll be following? Have you recorded all the names and numbers?

D. Have you considered the **durability** and maintenance of the items to be purchased?

E. Have you judged which optical illusions or **effects** the colors you have selected will have on each room? Reread Section 2 if you need help.

F. Do the colors you've selected follow this **formula** for room balance and harmony:

one + two + two = a perfect room

In other words, select:

One dominant or key color;

Two colors in lesser quantities; they can be different colors, or just different values — that is, tints or shades of the dominant color, as would be the case in a monochromatic, or one color scheme.

Two neutrals in any values (neutrals are white, black and brown).

G. **Go shopping for products with your color chips in hand.** Also remember to check the color of a product in the room where it will be used, in both artificial and daylight.

B. HOW TO MAKE AN EXTERIOR COLOR PLAN

Let's step outside and take a look at your home from across the street. How does it measure up?

Is the front door the focal point?

Is there a color that carries your eye from one side to the other?

Does it stand out from the house next door?

Does the landscape look manicured?

Would I give this home a second look?

If you answered no to any of the above — read on.

1. Photograph the area.

2. Enlarge it on a copier.

A ☆ BRIGHT IDEA!

JUST PICTURE IT!

While you're across the street, take a picture of your house (include all four sides) for future reference. Try the *Just Picture It!* idea as illustrated here (and also described in more detail on page 59) to help you "try on" new colors for your house before you actually start the project.

3. Outline every element with a black marker on white paper.

4. Color it in!

People rarely ever talk about it, but everyone sees it — the exterior of your home. What we mostly hear about is how to decorate the interior. Yet the exterior is just as important. Everyone sees it. The exterior is a clue to what's inside. It should say, "Welcome! Come on in!" The exterior of your home is a reflection of you and your lifestyle — something to be proud of.

If you are planning to sell your home . . . Remember, "as is" homes bring "as is" prices and bargain hunters.

The color of your house, no matter what color, is the color of money. A house with an attractive exterior has what realtors call "curb appeal" and that translates into value and a quick sale. No matter how charming and comfortable the inside of a home, if you can't get a buyer inside the door it will never be seen. Even if selling is the farthest thing from your mind, you'll want to keep your home well-maintained at all times — inside and outside.

Selecting exterior colors seems difficult for most people. As you know by now, color is tricky and changes with light. Natural light is uncontrollable, so you must control the color. For an accurate reading, select exterior colors outside on a cloudy, rather than sunny day. The color is truer with less contrast and fewer dark shadows. Walk the samples around all four sides of the house before you make a decision. Each side will probably look different, so don't set yourself up for a surprise by only taking a look at one side.

Unless you are building a home or replacing the roof and siding, you will have to work around these pre-existing elements. They will direct the selection of your paint colors. Follow the same steps as you did for the interior plans. Use your roof and facade as your starting point — match them to paint chips.

Make it easy on yourself and keep it simple. Mother Nature is on your side and provides you with an attractive backdrop of blue skies and green grass. In fact, don't forget to consider the color of your landscape. It is like a handsome frame that completes the picture. More on landscape later.

An attached garage door represents at least 40% of the exterior area of your home. Play it down. The front door should be the focal point.

COLORWIZE EXTERIOR WORDS

Roof The covering on top of your home. It includes everything from synthetic and wood shingles, to clay tiles, slate, and any other material that will do the trick.

Facade This is the "skin," or protective wrapper that covers the outside walls of the structure, and it can be made of all sorts of materials — wood, brick, aluminum, vinyl, concrete block, stone, cedar shakes, logs — any material that keeps the weather out.

Trim The finishing touches that dress up the exterior and tie the various elements together. It includes such things as the framing around doors and windows, the fascia boards (the board directly under the roof line), pillars and posts, porches, steps and railings. Trim can be made of a variety of materials and combinations.

Shutters Today, window shutters are more for ornamentation than function. They add decorative architectural detail to the style or character of the home. Shutters can also be a tool for visually widening a window or door while carrying color across the front of the house to maintain continuity and balance from one side to the other.

Front door This is the welcoming center and focal point of your home. It may consist of a number of materials in combination with glass or trim. Leave it natural or paint it a contrasting color for attention. Match your storm door to the color of the door.

Gutters, downspouts, milk chutes, and garage doors all fit into the category of "not to be seen." These are those functional things that aren't particularly attractive but necessary. A black downspout against a white facade, for instance, will stand out while creating a vertical cut down the side of the house. It also draws attention away from what should be getting the spotlight — the front door. Play these elements down. With the sweep of a paint brush, they can be blended into their background and magically disappear. Even if your garage is at the back of your lot, it should still blend with the facade.

Accents can include light fixtures, lamp posts, mailboxes, kick plates, house numbers, hardware, window boxes, and so on. Select them by *style* and *color* to contrast or blend into the background. They're the icing on the cake.

What's wrong with this picture? *Gutters, downspouts and garage door draw too much attention and give the home an unsettled, choppy appearance. See page 93.*

THREE SIMPLE EXTERIOR COLOR SCHEMES

A ONE COLOR (MONOCHROMATIC) SCHEME includes its various tints and shades. This scheme is the easiest to do. And because there is little contrast, it gives the home a smooth, relaxing and expanding look. It maintains harmony with different values of the same color.

a. Paint the shutters the dominant color of your roof.

b. Paint the front door a lighter tint of the color of your roof.

c. Paint or stain the wood trim a medium tone of your roof.

d. Paint the garage door, gutters and down spouts close to the tone of the shell of the house.

A TWO COLOR (NEIGHBORING) SCHEME draws a little more attention to detail. It softly highlights the features. Whatever the main color is, look for a second underlying color.

a. Squint at your home from across the street and draw out a color from the multicolor of your roof or facade.

b. Use this color for your second color on the wood trim; paint the shutters a little deeper so they stand out from the trim, and paint the front door like the dominant color in the roof. Again, paint gutters, garage doors and downspouts close to the color of the facade.

A CONTRASTING COLOR SCHEME draws the most attention to architectural details. Follow the instructions for a two color scheme except for the front door. Introduce a third color for contrast. Using the color wheel on the back of the book select a contrasting color that is opposite the color of your shutters or facade. For example, a red brick facade, #4 on the color wheel, with #9, 10, or 11 for the front door.

For simplification, you'll find a generic color chart below. The colors listed are the common family names instead of "given names." This is a very general representation. You'll need to do some work yourself. Always select colors by sight and on the 'site,' not by name. However, record your selections by manufacturer, given names, numbers and dye lots if available.

A GENERIC COLOR CHART

Roof	Body	Shutters	Door	Trim
dark gray	gray	charcoal	black or dark red	gray
light gray	white	charcoal	dark red or yellow	white
dark brown	beige	brown	dark green or yellow	gray
light brown	beige	brown	yellow	beige
black	gray	charcoal	dark red	gray
red	reddish brown	charcoal or deep blue	black or brick red	brown
green	beige	evergreen	light evergreen	off white
white	light gray or white	any muted color	any muted color	off white

MORE TIPS FOR SELECTING COLORS

- The best way to match the colors of permanent elements is to actually take a piece of brick, vinyl, shingle or whatever, shopping. In some cases that's virtually impossible. So try your best to find color chips that match. Perhaps you might take along a photograph of your home to help find the right color match.

- Review the maintenance, durability and finishes of exterior products and materials. Are they weather-proof and mildew resistant for your locality? Consider the direction your home faces. Colors fade the fastest on the south side of the house while the west and north sides bear the brunt of the weather. See more tips for the exterior in Section 5.

Purchase a pint of paint and try it on a small area first. Paint chips are too small to "tell the truth."

- To "try on" colors, paint a poster board and walk it around the house to see the color. Also view it from across the street. That's how it's really seen.

- The trend today is to show the beauty of natural wood. Many have chosen to stain front doors instead of painting them.

- We perceive deeper tones as being sturdy and showing strength. Therefore muted or greyed down tones look best for doors and trim. Bright vivid colors are best tolerated on homes in warm year-round climates. They reflect the heat and intense rays of the sun.

AN EXTERIOR CHECKLIST

Each home is different and these ideas are meant to be adapted to your individual situation. Use common sense and some ingenuity.

☑ **Contrast** is the key to emphasizing or high-lighting an element, and **blending** (with the background) is the key to camouflaging it.

☑ **Your front door is your focal point.** At a glance it should say "Welcome." Draw attention to it with color and then repeat that color in your flower beds and deciduous trees and shrubs, or add a colorful wreath to the door.

☑ **Window shutters are a secondary point** of focus. Even though they are not functional on most homes they are good for color balance. They carry color across the front of the house to unify the elements. They can also make windows and doors seem wider.

☑ **The garage door should take a back seat** to the front door. Blend it into the facade — especially if the garage is attached to a small house. If it is proportionally large in scale to your house, painting it a contrasting color will attract too much attention. Even if the garage sits at the back of the house, play it down. You are always safe painting it a deep beige with red brick — rather than red. Repeat the color on the trim.

☑ **Gutters, downspouts** and the like may be necessary parts of most homes, but they are by no means among the most attractive features. Best to choose a color that minimizes or camouflages them.

☑ **Extreme contrasts** can make a house look "hard." Black shutters on a snow white facade might be an example of this. It would be better to use a charcoal or deep gray for the shutters. If you must have black shutters, paint the house an off-white, beige or cream. Remember, deeper colors seem to show weight and strength.

Always use a deep or muted color rather than a light "whimsical" tone for the exterior color of a house. Deep colors look richer and project strength, weight, and sturdiness. A dark roof, for example, gives a home a strong sturdy look as compared to a light-colored roof.

Homes in warm climates are an excep- tion to the rule about deep, muted exterior colors. These homes need to use lighter colors to reflect the heat and light rays.

Always gray-down your trim, shutters, **and door accents.** Make them a little deeper and duller. For example, use a deep rich mustard gold instead of a bright daffodil yellow. Apply this rule to all exterior colors.

Another reason to select a little deeper **color** is that paint will eventually fade over a period of time, especially on the sides that face south and southwest.

To make a house look larger, paint it a light color, using a monochromatic scheme. The greater the unbroken expanse of color, the longer a house looks.

To hide or "remove" unsightly fea- **tures,** blend them with the color of their surroundings. Paint roof vents and exhaust fan exits, for example, the same color as the roof or facade.

To make a house look lower, create a horizontal line of color. A subtle contrast of color on the shutters or in the flower beds are examples. Sometimes a design in brick work or a change in material will do the trick — vinyl on the second level and brick on the bottom.

☑ **To make a house look taller** emphasize its vertical lines. For example, paint pillars and posts to stand out from the body of the house. Use a light neutral or contrasting color.

☑ **The exterior style of your home dictates** what is needed to maintain its integrity. Spanish tiles on a colonial style home would look out of place. Victorian homes need gingerbread details (fancy wood cut-outs). Most products are sold by style. Match hardware, light fixtures, and accessories to the style of the home.

☑ **Products should be selected to fit the proportions of your home.** For example, a narrow 3 1/4" vinyl or aluminum siding looks best on a smaller home, whereas a larger home can handle 6" slats. The narrow horizontal lines will give a small house a sleeker look. The same principle of proportion applies when adding trim or selecting stone or brick, decorative items, accessories, and even the size of an addition. They must fit the size of the home.

☑ **Heavy, rough-textured surfaces** look best on larger homes. As mentioned above, a smaller home cannot carry all that visual weight.

☑ **Shiny smooth finishes reflect light** and show every flaw. Dull ones absorb light. This applies not only when selecting paint finishes, but other products as well.

☑ **Always consider the climate** you live in, the natural environment and the quality of product needed to "weather the storm" in your geographic location.

Consider planting trees, bushes, and other landscaping with seasonal colors to match or contrast your house colors.

Examine colors in various light conditions before making a decision. Avoid paint color mistakes by purchasing a small amount and trying it out before you invest in more. Paint a good size area and study it on a cloudy day. Always stand back to observe the total picture...what a difference!

The care and upkeep of some products is minimal compared to others. Your time and maintenance costs are vital considerations. Ask questions before you purchase.

Plan ahead and improve the most important things first. Don't skimp on the things that are the most permanent. Shop price and quality as well as color.

A home can only hold the weight of two roofs. Carefully consider costs for removing the old ones before you add a new one.

Always get at least three estimates for any work to be done and a couple of references. The estimates shouldn't vary more than 10% either way and above all, be sure all bids are based on the same exact things. In fact, write up your own list of operations and specifications so that all bids are consistent. Don't forget that cleanup and hauling away debris can be a major cost issue in construction.

Now gather and view all your samples and study them together before ordering anything. Glue the actual samples into your color file and carry it with you or store it in the trunk of your car. You will always have it when you need it, now and for the future. You never need to make another color mistake.

DON'T FORGET ABOUT LANDSCAPING

- A well-planned landscape adds "spice" to your home. Flower beds lengthen the look of your home. They draw your eye from one side to the other.

- Before you paint, shingle or shutter, or put in new windows, think about the ABCs of color. Consider the **area**: do you want it to **blend** in for a harmonizing effect; or **contrast** it to add emphasis and attention?

- You can extend the length of your home by adding trees or shrubs at the corners. Repeat a color in at least three places.

- Use your landscaping for window privacy in some spots instead of a drapery.

- Strategically place a hedge or evergreen tree to keep direct sunlight out of your windows.

- Plant trees to naturally shade a patio or deck for evening enjoyment.

- To camouflage the view of a brick wall outside (or your neighbor's driveway), build a frame and install a sheet of 4' x 8' lattice. Place it 3' or 4' away from your window and plant any type of climbing vine you like.

- Ground covers can connect areas. Repeat the groupings to link a wide expanse.

- Tall trees can minimize the horizontal lines of a ranch home. They are an interesting contrast.

- Outline the pathway to your front door with a border of shrubs or flowers. They give depth to a home and lead the eye to the front door.

- Light, cool-colored flower beds enlarge space.

- To accent a feature of your home introduce a contrasting colored tree or bush. An unusual shape or foliage texture adds to its character.

- Don't forget the white picket fence for a bungalow or a natural split-rail for a more rustic look.

- If you live in the North, think of colors for winter. Use some evergreens to contrast with the snow.

- To give your property depth, plant a colorful or evergreen tree in the center of your front lawn, equidistant from the home and public walk.

Don't cut those trees. Just trim them. Mature trees can add up to 15% to the value of a home.

Looking back at page 84, here's a better look. *The front door is the focal point. The landscaping also enhances and extends the length of the home while softening the corners.*

C. CHARTING COLORS FOR A BRAND NEW HOME

For more variety in a home, each room can vary by scheme, depending upon the level of activity the room is used for. A **monochromatic scheme,** which uses one slice out of the color wheel, will do nicely in a room for solitude. A **neighboring scheme,** using two or three slices next to each other, is appropriate for a moderate level of activity, whereas a **contrasting scheme,** which uses any wedges directly across from each other, is best for a high-energy room. Remember to keep weaving a key color throughout the house.

Simply follow steps 1 - 4 on pages 71-80. Pick up two paint color chips for each color you're using; one to glue onto the chip chart shown on the next page, and another to distribute onto your floor plans. You might find it helpful to review Section 2, to make sure you're remembering the special effects of color.

Once you fill in the chip chart, turn the page and you can begin to distribute each of these colors onto your floor plan to represent the wall, ceiling, floor colors and wood trim. The colors for furniture, window coverings and accents will fall into place because you have the basic colors.

- Keep the size of the room and its use in mind to help determine whether you want to use tints to increase its size or deeper shades to create drama or coziness.

- Consider whether you want warm or cool colors to dominate the room. Study the direction the house faces for rooms to enjoy the sun rise or set.

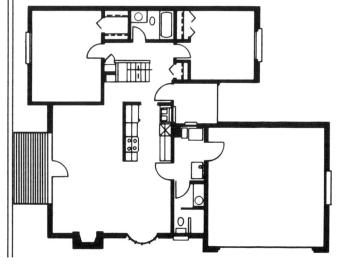

Use this color chart with a ready-made scheme or your favorite colors from the color wheel (see page 69).

COLORS   TINTS AND SHADES

1.

2.

3.

4.

NEUTRALS

Example of a

FLOOR PLAN FOR
COLOR DISTRIBUTION

The idea here is to make each room different by flip-flopping a dominant color in one room to become an accent color in the next and so on. This is also the time to consider the "special effects" of color and the rooms that will be getting the most sun. Review Section 2, *The Tricky Side of Color.*

You can use a fabric sample as your guide.

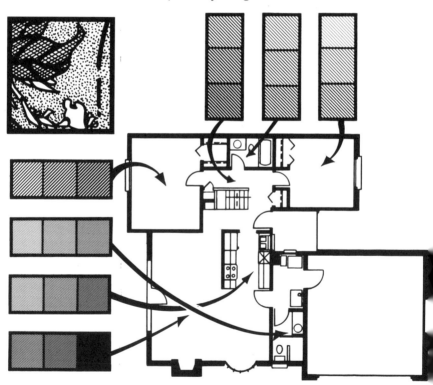

Once this step is complete you can begin shopping for the actual products to match the room colors. Use the pages in Section 6 to glue in the actual swatches and samples of carpeting, laminates, fabrics, etc.

DISTRIBUTING COLORS
FOR A BRAND-NEW HOME

Glue color samples on these pages or right on your floor plan, as in the diagram on page 96. Ceilings and trim will most likely be the same throughout.

	FLOOR	CEILING	WALLS	TRIM
FOYER				
KITCHEN				
BATH #1				
BATH #2				
DINING RM.				
LIVING RM.				
LIBRARY/DEN				
FAMILY/ MEDIA ROOM				

more on next page

	FLOOR	CEILING	WALLS	TRIM
GREAT ROOM				
LAUNDRY ROOM				
MASTER BEDROOM				
MASTER BATH				
BEDROOM #1				
BEDROOM #2				
BEDROOM #3				
BATH #3				
OTHER				

ARRANGING FURNITURE

Early on in your planning it's a good idea to plan where your furniture will be placed. It helps to see where you may want to put extra spotlights, a chandelier or track lighting and perhaps some additional electrical outlets.

- Work out comfortable traffic patterns and leg room for kitchen chairs and living room sofas.

- Keep heat ducts clear for maximum efficiency.

- Remember to consider the natural light in the rooms on the "sunny side" of the street to keep color from fading. This can be done inside with window coverings or outside with shade trees.

STEPS FOR PLACING YOUR FURNITURE

a. Measure your furniture and draw templates of each piece on index cards (1/4 inch equals a foot). Cut them out and move them around on your graph paper floor plan until you find a comfortable arrangement. You may wish to use the templates and graph paper provided in Section 6.

b. Begin by selecting a focal point in your room. It can be a bay or picture window, a fireplace, a painting on the wall, the entertainment center, or just a particular area where you want to set your furniture.

c. For a conversational grouping, visually create a square or rectangle in front of the focal point and set the furniture within that space. Set in the largest piece of furniture first, followed by the smaller pieces. Re-

member to leave enough space for walking
and stretching your legs. Form follows function!

d. Now fill the remaining spaces around the
    room with smaller pieces of furniture. If the
    room is large enough, create another con-
    versational grouping.

e. For a fresh look, try a diagonal arrange-
    ment. Set the visual square diagonally to
    the room's focal point.

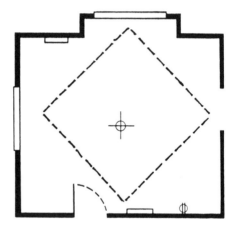

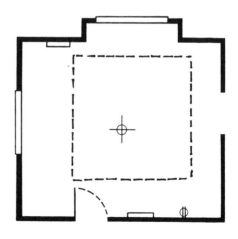

MORE TIPS AND TRICKS

- Before you begin building bookshelves and cabinets, make sure they are where you need them. On a quiet Sunday afternoon when there are no workmen around, take a couple of lawn chairs to the house and sit in each room to get a feel for where you want to put your furniture for the best views and traffic patterns and where you might want your built-ins.

- It's also a good idea to lay out your furniture arrangement before you begin putting in the electrical wiring for fixtures, cable and phone systems.

- For energy conservation, consider ceiling fans for two-story rooms to circulate the air efficiently. Also consider tinted or insulated glass windows for sun and temperature control.

- Think about contrast when it comes to selecting the color of electrical outlets, fans, the trim on skylights, and the rims of recessed or track lighting.

- Contrast draws attention. Keep the unimportant things inconspicuous; select a color that will match the wall color. The same goes for switch plates and fans.

- Unity in a home is achieved by the color flow from room to room. The same color floor coverings and woodwork throughout helps, especially if rooms open into each other.

- Even without moving furniture, you can get a life-size idea of furniture placement and traffic patterns. Try this: Measure and layout sheets of newspaper on the floor to approximate the size and position of each piece.

For harmony either in a small or large home you can keep the floor colors or the wood trim the same throughout. This doesn't mean the same texture or finish. It can go from carpeting to tile, to vinyl, to wood. The common denominator is the color.

"Uncolors," such as white, black or brown can be used in any value. They blend nicely with any color scheme. In fact, they are good stable colors that enhance and tie the room together. The natural wood on your furniture, floors or trim is considered a neutral.

⭐ WHEN YOU NEED A BREAK!

Just for fun, if you need a break, rent the video, "Mr. Blandings Builds His Dream House," (starring Cary Grant). You'll easily be able to relate to it.

5
FIFTY-NIFTY
TIPS AT A
GLANCE

A Quick Review Of
The Tips, Tricks And
Color Traps

FIFTY-NIFTY MONEY-SAVING TIPS, TRICKS & COLOR TRAPS TO AVOID

COLOR

1. **Color is free, and the choices are up to you.** Color is part of everything we purchase. It costs no more to select and blend the right colors, than it does to end up with mismatched lackluster combinations. That's when it becomes costly. Because color is tricky, learn all you can before you shop.

2. **Light is what gives us the pleasure of color,** but also the trouble. Make all color decisions in the light setting it will appear in. Take home the largest sample possible to avoid 'color surprises' later.

3. **Color can create illusions.** It can change our moods from relaxed to edgy, make a room feel warm or cool, and even alter its size, visually.

4. **The Color Wheel** (see back cover) is your tool to *Making Color Work.* It's the key to what goes with what. It contains the colors of the rainbow. Like a pie, it is divided into 12 wedges of colors, each showing its tint or pastel color and a deeper shade. You can match your existing colors to any wedges and create a new scheme by pulling out one, two or three wedges. Here is how to do it:
Take any one slice out of the pie for a **monochromatic** scheme. This is a one-color scheme that can include as many of its tints and shades as you wish. It is easy

to do, the most relaxing and the best for expanding space — especially when using light colors. One example of this scheme is wedge #2, or any one other wedge by itself.

Pick any two or three wedges either side of a color and you have a **neighboring** scheme. An example would be wedges 5, 6, and 7. This scheme is more colorful and active looking.

For drama and contrast, select wedges directly across from each other. This is known as a **complementary, or contrasting** scheme. It contains both warm and cool colors. It has an outgoing personality. An example would be wedge #2 with #8, or even #2 with #8 and #9.

5. **Cool colors: blue, green, and purple,** are sometimes referred to as evening colors. They are conservative and more formal than warm colors. Both warm and cool colors can be used together for an active atmosphere. This is called a *complementary* or *contrasting* color scheme. Use the color wedges directly across from each other on the color wheel. **Warm colors: red, yellow, and orange,** are called daytime colors. They are full of the sun's energy, less formal and more lively. They give a sense of hospitality.

6. **Bright colors, such as shocking pink, draw attention** and become tiring in large quantities. Use them wisely — to suit the purpose.

7. **Pastels or tints are colors that have been mixed with white.** They give a sense of spaciousness, while shades, their deeper counterparts which

are mixed with black, do the opposite.

8. **Dark colors give things a sense of weight, strength or stability.** If two boxes of the same size were painted differently, one black and one white, which one would you think weighed less? You're right, the white one. Remember this when selecting exterior colors and furniture for small rooms.

9. **Dark-colored rooms can be perked up** with accents of light colors. Just painting the wood trim an off-white will do the trick.

10. **Grayed or muted colors are more calming** than pure colors. Avoid mixing the two in the same room. The muted ones will look faded or worn next to the pure colors. This is what color intensity is all about.

11. **Before making any purchase,** always ask yourself whether you want the item to blend or contrast with the rest of your decor. Contrast draws attention and blending does the opposite.

A SIMPLE COLOR PLAN

12. **Make it easy on yourself and adapt a color plan** that has already been put together by a designer. Select an attractive scarf, tie, fabric, wallpaper or a favorite object that contains the colors you like, and use it as your guide. Take it to a paint store and match the colors to paint chips. Take them home and distribute the colors as follows.Keep in mind the special effects or optical illusions color can create. Always use unequal amounts of color. Se-

lect one to be the key color and then use the others in lesser amounts.

a. Pull out one of the colors from your chips to use on the walls as a background.

b. Use the same color in a different value for the floor covering, or choose the next deepest color from the color chips.

c. For the furniture, select the next deepest color. It can be a patterned fabric that includes all the colors from your adapted design.

d. To add sparkle to the room, use the strongest of the colors for your accessories, and smaller pieces of furniture.

MATCHING COLORS OF HARD-TO-GET-AT ITEMS

13. If you're shopping to match the color of some existing pieces of furniture, fixed elements, bath fixtures or things too large to carry, here are some suggestions:

• Bring some paint chips or stain samples home that you think might match.

• Take a small drawer with you.

• Take an arm chair cover or sofa cushion.

• Snip some carpet fibers from a closet or corner and glue them onto a card.

• Clip a strip of fabric from a seam under the sofa or drapery seam and attach it to another index card.

• Find something in the house that matches the immovable piece and take it shopping as your guide. Use your imagination! A spool of thread, a colored pencil, or even a crayon might work.

14. Here's a formula for a perfect room using an adapted plan or creating one from the color wheel: 1+2+2.

1 = Select **one** dominant, or key color.

2 = Select **two** colors to be used in lesser quantities (they can be different than the dominant color, or just different values, that is, tints or shades of the dominant color).

2 = Select **two** neutrals in any values (neutrals are white, black and brown).

COLOR BALANCE

15. Repeat an accent color (in different values) at least two more times in a room, for unity and balance. Introduce it in patterned fabrics, picture mats, lampshades, pillows or other accessories.

CONNECTING ROOMS WITH COLOR

16. Use various values of a key color throughout your home. This is especially important to unify or visually enlarge a small home or spaces that open into each other. For example, keep the walls or floors or even the wood trim the same color.

SHOPPING FOR COLOR

17. Cinnamon toast, strawberry jam and mandarin orange ... are you ordering breakfast or carpeting? Don't be swayed, or order anything by color name alone. "Seeing is believing." Names and numbers change with every manufacturer.

PAINT

18. Paints come in different finishes. The more sheen, the more light it reflects. Higher sheens seem to draw more attention to uneven or defective walls Use carefully. However, they are most washable.

Types of finishes:
>   Flat = a matte finish with no sheen.
>   Eggshell = slight sheen finish.
>   Satin = moderate sheen finish.
>   Semi-Gloss = more sheen.
>   High Gloss = highly reflective, super sheen.

Flat and eggshell are popular for most walls and satin for wood trim.

19. Dark paints dry lighter, and light colors dry darker, so don't panic! Be patient.

20. Walls reflect off of each other, so colors can end up looking more intense than you may have expected them to. You may want to select something a little lighter for walls.

21. Square off a long narrow room or hallway by painting the two short walls a deeper shade of the color of the long walls.

PATTERNS

22. Small patterns are best for small areas whether it be on the walls, furniture, window coverings or carpeting. Be especially careful in kitchens and baths that are "cut up" with cabinets, fixtures and windows. Patterns give life to a room — don't be afraid to use them.

23. Large pieces of furniture and large rooms can carry a larger print wallpaper and fabric design. In general, remember to keep everything in scale to the proportions of the room, e.g. small furniture for small rooms and vice versa.

MIXING AND MATCHING PATTERNS

24. When matching patterns in a room, the common denominator is color. In other words, one key color should be a part of each pattern.

25. When mixing patterns, work in opposites. Mix large patterns with small ones, plaids with stripes, florals with checks, checks with stripes, pin-dots with stripes and so on.

26. Always use unequal amounts of patterns in each room for interest.

27. When it comes to color, patterns and their placement, think of a room as a teeter-totter. Balance the placement of these elements to carry the eye comfortably across the room. For example, two small blue patterned chairs can be balanced by a tweed sofa or a solid blue one across the room. The piping on the sofa could connect them; or maybe the colors in the throw pillows, a picture, or lamp–shades.

TEXTURES

28. Textures give character to a room. They add warmth, and it happens naturally. For example, your carpeting or wood floors are of a different texture than your

110

walls, and of course, so are your fabrics.

29. Heavy textures look best on larger pieces of furniture or areas; finer textures are most appropriate for smaller pieces.

30. Don't mix a very fine texture with a heavy texture. For example, a fine silk drapery next to a brick wall is too extreme.

31. When trying to match colors of different textures there will probably be a variance. Since more light reflects off a smooth surface than it does a rougher one, a color match will rarely look exact. That's okay. Stand back and look at it from a distance. That's how you'd naturally live with them anyway.

32. A room can easily be decorated with up to three different colors. Remember, there are hundreds of shades and tints of each that can be used. Did you know that the human eye can discern up to 10 million colors? It's amazing to think that it all begins with three primary colors: red, yellow and blue plus black and white. Now that's magic!

WALLPAPER TONIC

33. Come home with wallpaper, instead of frazzled nerves or a headache. Here's a check list to review before you walk out the door:
   a. Measure the room and openings.
   b. Gather up your paint colors, fabric samples and this book.
   c. Decide on a style. Is the room traditional, contemporary or somewhere

in-between?

d. Do you need something scrubbable for the kitchen or bath?

e. Do you want something prepasted, and who is going to install it?

f. Do you want a plaid, stripe, floral, animals or something such as a sport or circus theme?

g. Do you want this wallpaper to visually alter the space in any way?

- A light colored background will open the space.
- An all-over deep colored pattern will add drama or coziness.
- Vertical stripes lift the ceiling.
- Horizontal stripes or a border at the ceiling will visually lower it.
- A diagonal pattern gives the walls more depth.

AT THE WALLPAPER SHOP

34. **Ask if the wallpaper books are organized** in any manner. Some shops stack their books on the shelf by room, style, textures, stripes, borders or certain designers.

35. **Sometimes the design and colors on the cover or title** of the book is a clue to what's inside. Once you have the book in front of you:

a. Quickly flip through the papers at the corner to find the color section you need.

b. Open to that section and begin matching your chips and fabrics to the paper. (Check out the source of light. You may want to step outside for a better match.)

c. Select only three books to take home at a time. More is confusing.

BACK HOME AGAIN

36. Study the samples in view of all the other elements in the room for at least a day or two.

37. Once you decide, carefully copy all the information from the back of the page, book title and manufacturer.

38. Remember to always check the dye lot number of every roll once it is delivered. Keep the numbers handy in case you need to order more. Dye lots can be different. In fact, it's a good idea to keep an extra roll on hand for future repairs.

39. If you're having trouble making a decision, go back and get three more books.

40. Ask about ordering one roll or a large enough sample to tape on your wall before you decide.

41. Know there is a difference in quantity per roll depending on whether it is an American or European roll.

FURNITURE ARRANGING

42. a. Begin by selecting a focal point in your room. It can be a bay or picture window, a fireplace, a painting on the wall or just a particular area where you want to set your furniture.

b. As mentioned earlier, draw templates of your furniture on index cards (1/4 inch equals a foot). Cut them out and move them around on the graph paper that shows the floor plan. See page 202 for samples of templates.

c. Visually create a square or rectangle in front of the focal point and set the furniture within that space. For a conversational grouping, set in the largest piece of furniture first, followed by the smaller pieces. Remember to leave enough space for walking and stretching your legs. Form follows function!

d. Now fill the remaining space around the room with smaller pieces. If the room is large enough, create another conversational grouping or add a writing desk or chair and a reading lamp or even a group of plants.

43. If your room is large enough you may want to try setting the visual square diagonally to the focal point.

44. Give your furniture some breathing space. Always keep it at least 3" to 6" away from the walls. It actually makes a room look larger — it's an optical illusion — try it, you'll be surprised.

THE EXTERIOR

45. Before you decide on colors, take a drive to get a look at other homes and gather some ideas. Take pictures of the ones you like. A bright idea is to take a picture of your home, enlarge it on a copy machine, trace the outline on tracing paper and color it in, trying different color combinations. Reread: *Just Picture It,* on page 59

THREE COMMON
EXTERIOR COLOR SCHEMES

46. We all use paint as a protective finish on our exterior. But also think of it as a way to highlight and spruce up your home. Color has become the key to adding value and charm both inside and out.

A ONE COLOR (MONOCHROMATIC) SCHEME includes its various tints and shades. This scheme is the easiest to do. And because there is little contrast, it gives the home a smooth, relaxing and expanding look. It maintains harmony with different values of the same color.

a. paint the shutters the dominant color of your roof.

b. paint the front door a lighter tint of the color of your roof.

c. paint or stain the wood trim a medium tone of your roof.

d. paint the garage door, gutters and down spouts as close to the tone of the shell of the house.

A TWO COLOR (NEIGHBORING) SCHEME draws a little more attention to detail. It softly highlights the features. Whatever the main color is, look for a second underlying color.

a. squint at your home from across the street and draw out a color from the multicolor of your roof or facade.

b. Use this color for your second color on the wood trim; paint the shutters a little deeper so they stand out from the trim, and paint the front door like the dominant color in the roof. Again, paint gutters, garage doors and downspouts close to the color of the facade.

A CONTRASTING COLOR SCHEME
draws the most attention to architectural details. Follow the instructions for a two color scheme except for the front door. Introduce a third color for contrast. Using the color wheel on the back of the book select a contrasting color that is opposite the color of your shutters.

47. **Contrasting garage doors, gutters and downspouts will only emphasize them.** You may not want to draw attention to them. Your front door is the welcoming center and should be the focal point.

48. **Always use muted or grayed down colors on the exterior of your home** if you live in the north. Deep colors show strength and stability. Bright or pastel colors look too whimsical. However, the further south you go and the hotter the climate, lighter and brighter colors become necessary to reflect the hot sun. Homes should nestle into their natural geographical environment.

49. **If your home is a declared historical site,** or a new home that mimics a historical style, maintain its integrity by selecting paint colors from a historical paint color chart.

50. **White is always a good bet to trim your home.** However, if you are repainting, select one that is not pure white. It's too 'contrasty' for most homes, unless the brick or siding is white. Select something that has a little beige in it. It will give your home a heartier, softer, richer look.

116

6

YOUR COLORING
WORKBOOK

Swatch Sheets And
Chip Charts, Floor
Plans And Furniture
Templates

INTERIOR

This workbook section goes hand and hand with Section 4, What Goes With What and How.

The following pages are provided for recording and gluing in interior and exterior colors and samples for planning and shopping. Furniture templates are at the end of this section.

STEP 1

Room Measurements and graph paper for floor plans.

STEP 2

Notes, ideas, styles, themes and photos, so you can be sure to record all names, numbers, codes and dye lots of each item and even phone numbers and contacts.

STEP 3

Space to glue in your color chips.

STEP 4

Space to glue in the actual samples of the materials and swatches for carpeting, counters, cabinets, shingles, fabrics, and even the kitchen sink!

STEP 1

Measurements: **FOYER/ENTRANCE**

Length _____ x Width _____ = Square feet _____

Ceiling Height = _____

Entrance door	Length	Width	Depth
_____	_____	_____	_____

Inside front door	Length	Width	Depth
_____	_____	_____	_____

Windows	Length	Width	Depth
_____	_____	_____	_____

Other	Length	Width	Depth
_____	_____	_____	_____
_____	_____	_____	_____
_____	_____	_____	_____

NOTES:

STEP 1
Floor and furniture plans: **FOYER/ENTRANCE**

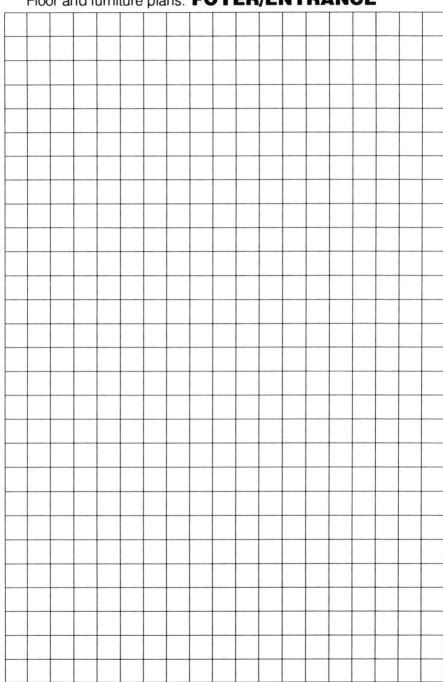

scale: 1/4 inch = 1 foot

STEP 2
FOYER/ENTRANCE
notes • ideas • photos • pictures • furniture

Type of Scheme: ❑ One color (one wedge of the color wheel)

❑ Neighboring (2 or 3 wedges side by side)

❑ Contrasting (opposite wedges)

Type of Style: ❑ Traditional, Country, Victorian

❑ Contemporary, Eclectic

===== Contacts, phone numbers, product information: =====

STEP 3
FOYER/ENTRANCE COLOR CHART

Wall Color	Wood Trim	Ceiling
Floor Color	Tile Color	Wood or Vinyl Color

Window Covering Color

Other

Furniture Wood Color

Fabric Color

Hardware & Accessories

Wall Covering

Wood Trim

Ceiling

Floor Covering

Tile Piece

Wood Floor Stain or Vinyl

Window Fabric

Other

Furniture Stain

Fabric Swatch

Hardware & Accessories

Record names, numbers, dye lots and codes

STEP 1

Measurements: **KITCHEN**

Length _____ x Width _____ = Square feet _____
Ceiling Height = _____

Appliances	Length	Width	Depth
_____	_____	_____	_____
_____	_____	_____	_____
_____	_____	_____	_____

Cabinets	Length	Width	Depth
_____	_____	_____	_____
_____	_____	_____	_____

Counter Tops	Length	Width	Depth
_____	_____	_____	_____
_____	_____	_____	_____

Windows	Length	Width	Depth
_____	_____	_____	_____
_____	_____	_____	_____

Entrance doors	Length	Width	Depth
_____	_____	_____	_____
_____	_____	_____	_____

Other	Length	Width	Depth
_____	_____	_____	_____
_____	_____	_____	_____
_____	_____	_____	_____

NOTES:

STEP 1
Floor and furniture plans: **KITCHEN**

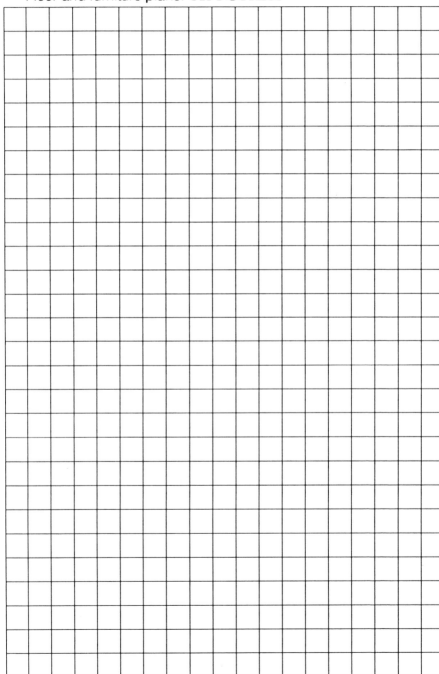

126

scale: 1/4 inch = 1 foot

STEP 2

KITCHEN
notes • ideas • photos • pictures • furniture

Type of Scheme: ❏ One color (one wedge of the color wheel)

❏ Neighboring (2 or 3 wedges side by side)

❏ Contrasting (opposite wedges)

Type of Style: ❏ Traditional, Country, Victorian

❏ Contemporary, Eclectic

═══ Contacts, phone numbers, product information: ═══

STEP 3
KITCHEN COLOR CHIP CHART

Wall Color

Wood Trim

Ceiling

Floor Color

Tile Color

Wood or Vinyl Color

Appliances Color

Cabinet Color

Counter Color

Sink Color

Hardware & Accessories

Window Covering Color

Other

Furniture Wood Color

Fabric Color

Wall Covering

Wood Trim

Ceiling

Floor Covering

Tile Piece

Wood Floor Stain or Vinyl

Appliance Color

Cabinet Finish

Counter Top Sample

Sink Color

Hardware & Accessories

Window Fabric

Other

Furniture Stain

Fabric Swatch

STEP 1
Measurements: **DINING ROOM**

Length _____ x Width _____ = Square feet _____

Ceiling Height = _____

Windows	Length	Width	Depth
_____	_____	_____	_____
_____	_____	_____	_____

Doors	Length	Width	Depth
_____	_____	_____	_____
_____	_____	_____	_____

Other	Length	Width	Depth
_____	_____	_____	_____
_____	_____	_____	_____
_____	_____	_____	_____

NOTES:

STEP 1

Floor and furniture plans: **DINING ROOM**

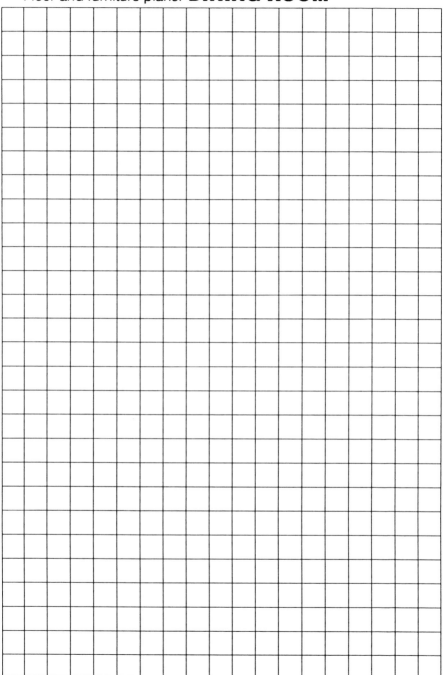

scale: 1/4 inch = 1 foot

STEP 2
DINING ROOM
notes • ideas • photos • pictures • furniture

Type of Scheme: ❑ One color (one wedge of the color wheel)

❑ Neighboring (2 or 3 wedges side by side)

❑ Contrasting (opposite wedges)

Type of Style: ❑ Traditional, Country, Victorian

❑ Contemporary, Eclectic

===== Contacts, phone numbers, product information: =====

STEP 3
DINING ROOM COLOR CHART

Wall Color   Wood Trim   Ceiling

Floor Color   Tile Color   Wood or Vinyl Color

Hardware & Accessories

Window Covering Color   Other

Furniture Wood Color   Fabric Colors

Wall Covering

Wood Trim

Ceiling

Floor Covering

Tile Piece

Wood Floor Stain or Vinyl

Hardware & Accessories

Window Fabric

Other

Furniture Stain

Main Fabric Swatch

More Fabrics

STEP 1

Measurements: **BATHROOM 1**

Length _____ x Width _____ = Square feet _____

Ceiling Height = _____

Bath Fixtures	Length	Width	Depth
tub/shower	_____	_____	_____
toilet	_____	_____	_____
sink	_____	_____	_____

Cabinets	Length	Width	Depth
_____	_____	_____	_____
_____	_____	_____	_____

Counter Tops	Length	Width	Depth
_____	_____	_____	_____
_____	_____	_____	_____

Windows	Length	Width	Depth
_____	_____	_____	_____
_____	_____	_____	_____

Doors	Length	Width	Depth
_____	_____	_____	_____
_____	_____	_____	_____

Other	Length	Width	Depth
_____	_____	_____	_____
_____	_____	_____	_____
_____	_____	_____	_____

NOTES:

STEP 1

Floor and furniture plans: **BATHROOM 1**

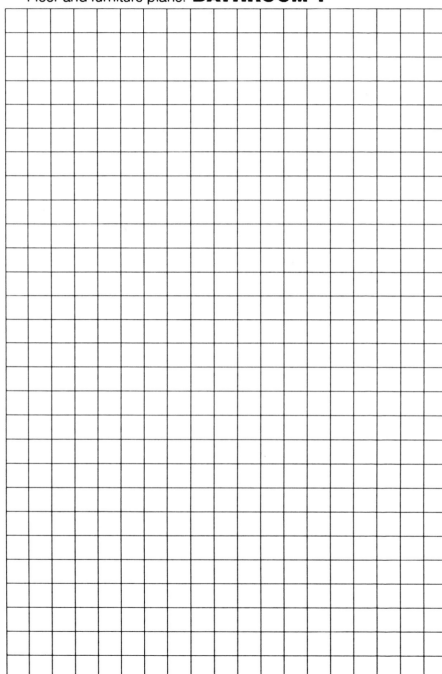

138

scale: 1/4 inch = 1 foot

STEP 2

BATHROOM 1
notes • ideas • photos • pictures • furniture

Type of Scheme: ❑ One color (one wedge of the color wheel)

❑ Neighboring (2 or 3 wedges side by side)

❑ Contrasting (opposite wedges)

Type of Style: ❑ Traditional, Country, Victorian

❑ Contemporary, Eclectic

═══ Contacts, phone numbers, product information: ═══

STEP 3
BATHROOM 1 COLOR CHART

Wall Color	Wood Color	Ceiling Color
Floor Color	Tile Color	Counter Color
Sink/Tub Color	Cabinets	Window Cover Color
Shower Curtain Color	Hardware Color	Other
	Accessories	

Wall Covering	Wood Trim	Ceiling
Floor Tile Piece	Wall Tile Piece	Counter Top
Sink	Toilet	Tub
Window Cover	Shower Curtain	Hardware
Other & Accessories		

STEP 1

Measurements: **LAUNDRY**

Length _____ x Width _____ = Square feet _____
Ceiling Height = _____

Appliances	Length	Width	Depth
_____	_____	_____	_____
_____	_____	_____	_____
_____	_____	_____	_____

Cabinets	Length	Width	Depth
_____	_____	_____	_____
_____	_____	_____	_____

Counter Tops	Length	Width	Depth
_____	_____	_____	_____
_____	_____	_____	_____

Windows	Length	Width	Depth
_____	_____	_____	_____
_____	_____	_____	_____

Entrance doors	Length	Width	Depth
_____	_____	_____	_____
_____	_____	_____	_____

Other	Length	Width	Depth
_____	_____	_____	_____
_____	_____	_____	_____
_____	_____	_____	_____

NOTES:

STEP 1
Floor and furniture plans: **LAUNDRY**

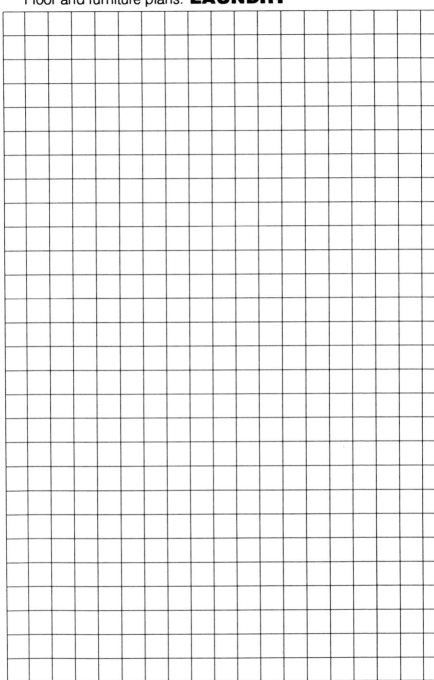

scale: 1/4 inch = 1 fo

STEP 2

LAUNDRY
notes • ideas • photos • pictures • furniture

Type of Scheme: ❏ One color (one wedge of the color wheel)

❏ Neighboring (2 or 3 wedges side by side)

❏ Contrasting (opposite wedges)

Type of Style: ❏ Traditional, Country, Victorian

❏ Contemporary, Eclectic

===== Contacts, phone numbers, product information: =====

STEP 3
LAUNDRY COLOR CHART

Wall Color

Wood Trim

Ceiling

Floor Color

Tile Color

Wood or Vinyl Color

Appliance Color

Cabinet Color

Counter Color

Sink Color

Hardware & Accessories

Window Covering Color

Other

Furniture Wood Color

Fabric Color

LAUNDRY

STEP 4 • SAMPLES

Wall Covering

Wood Trim

Ceiling

Floor Covering

Tile Piece

Wood Floor Stain or Vinyl

Appliance Color

Cabinet Finish

Counter Top Sample

Tub/Sink Color

Hardware & Accessories

Window Fabric

Other

Record names, numbers, dye lots and codes

STEP 1

Measurements: **LIVING ROOM**

Length _____ x Width _____ = Square feet _____

Ceiling Height = _____

Cabinets	Length	Width	Depth
_____	_____	_____	_____
_____	_____	_____	_____

Counter Tops	Length	Width	Depth
_____	_____	_____	_____
_____	_____	_____	_____

Windows	Length	Width	Depth
_____	_____	_____	_____
_____	_____	_____	_____

Doors	Length	Width	Depth
_____	_____	_____	_____
_____	_____	_____	_____

Other	Length	Width	Depth
_____	_____	_____	_____
_____	_____	_____	_____
_____	_____	_____	_____

NOTES:

STEP 1

Floor and furniture plans: **LIVING ROOM**

scale: 1/4 inch = 1 foo

STEP 2
LIVING ROOM
notes • ideas • photos • pictures • furniture

Type of Scheme: ❏ One color (one wedge of the color wheel)

❏ Neighboring (2 or 3 wedges side by side)

❏ Contrasting (opposite wedges)

Type of Style: ❏ Traditional, Country, Victorian

❏ Contemporary, Eclectic

═══ Contacts, phone numbers, product information: ═══

STEP 3
LIVING ROOM COLOR CHART

Wall Color   Wood Trim   Ceiling

Floor Color   Tile Color   Wood or Vinyl Color

Appliance Color   Cabinet Color   Counter Color

Hardware & Accessories

Window Covering Color   Other

Furniture Wood Color   Fabric Colors

Wall Covering

Wood Trim

Ceiling

Floor Covering

Tile Piece

Wood Floor Stain or Vinyl

Hardware & Accessories

Window Fabric

Other

Furniture Stain

Main Fabric Swatch

More Fabrics

STEP 1

Measurements: **FAMILY/MEDIA ROOM**

Length _____ x Width _____ = Square feet _____
Ceiling Height = _____

Cabinets	Length	Width	Depth
_____	_____	_____	_____
_____	_____	_____	_____

Counter Tops	Length	Width	Depth
_____	_____	_____	_____
_____	_____	_____	_____

Windows	Length	Width	Depth
_____	_____	_____	_____
_____	_____	_____	_____

Doors	Length	Width	Depth
_____	_____	_____	_____
_____	_____	_____	_____

Built-ins	Length	Width	Depth
_____	_____	_____	_____
_____	_____	_____	_____
_____	_____	_____	_____

NOTES:

STEP 1
Floor and furniture plans: **FAMILY/MEDIA ROOM**

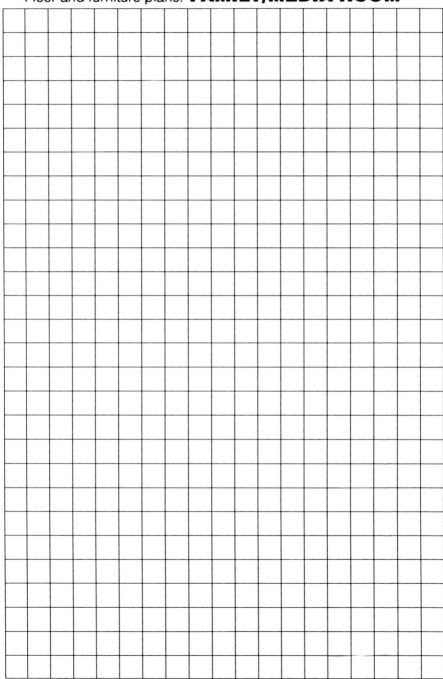

scale: 1/4 inch = 1 foot

STEP 2
FAMILY/MEDIA ROOM
notes • ideas • photos • pictures • furniture

Type of Scheme: ❑ One color (one wedge of the color wheel)

❑ Neighboring (2 or 3 wedges side by side)

❑ Contrasting (opposite wedges)

Type of Style: ❑ Traditional, Country, Victorian

❑ Contemporary, Eclectic

===== Contacts, phone numbers, product information: =====

STEP 3
FAMILY/MEDIA COLOR CHART

Wall Color	Wood Trim	Ceiling

Floor Color	Tile Color	Wood or Vinyl Color

Appliance Color	Cabinet Color	Counter Color

Hardware & Accessories

Window Covering Color   Other

Furniture Wood Color   Fabric Colors

STEP 4 • SAMPLES

Wall Covering

Wood Trim

Ceiling

Floor Covering

Tile Piece

Wood Floor Stain or Vinyl

Hardware & Accessories

Window Fabric

Other

Furniture Stain

Main Fabric Swatch

More Fabrics

STEP 1

Measurements: **LIBRARY/DEN**

Length _____ x Width _____ = Square feet _____

Ceiling Height = _____

Cabinets	Length	Width	Depth
_____	_____	_____	_____
_____	_____	_____	_____

Counter Tops	Length	Width	Depth
_____	_____	_____	_____
_____	_____	_____	_____

Windows	Length	Width	Depth
_____	_____	_____	_____
_____	_____	_____	_____

Doors	Length	Width	Depth
_____	_____	_____	_____
_____	_____	_____	_____

OTHER	Length	Width	Depth
_____	_____	_____	_____
_____	_____	_____	_____
_____	_____	_____	_____

NOTES:

STEP 1
Floor and furniture plans: **LIBRARY/DEN**

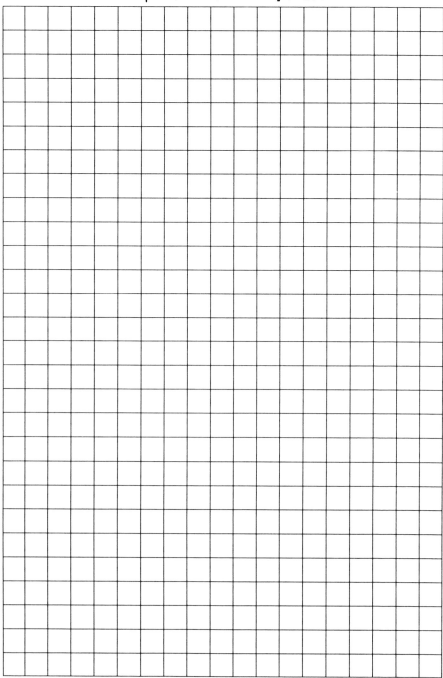

scale: 1/4 inch = 1 foot

STEP 2
LIBRARY/DEN
notes • ideas • photos • pictures • furniture

Type of Scheme: ☐ One color (one wedge of the color wheel)

☐ Neighboring (2 or 3 wedges side by side)

☐ Contrasting (opposite wedges)

Type of Style: ☐ Traditional, Country, Victorian

☐ Contemporary, Eclectic

===== Contacts, phone numbers, product information: =====

STEP 3
LIBRARY/DEN COLOR CHART

Wall Color   Wood Trim   Ceiling

Floor Color   Tile Color   Wood or Vinyl Color

Appliance Color   Cabinet Color   Counter Color

Hardware & Accessories

Window Covering Color   Other

Furniture Wood Color   Fabric Colors

164

Wall Covering

Wood Trim

Ceiling

Floor Covering

Tile Piece

Wood Floor Stain or Vinyl

Hardware & Accessories

Window Fabric

Other

Furniture Stain

Main Fabric Swatch

More Fabrics

STEP 1
Measurements: **BEDROOM 1**

Length _____ x Width _____ = Square feet _____

Ceiling Height = _____

Windows	Length	Width	Depth
_____	_____	_____	_____
_____	_____	_____	_____

Doors	Length	Width	Depth
_____	_____	_____	_____
_____	_____	_____	_____

OTHER	Length	Width	Depth
_____	_____	_____	_____
_____	_____	_____	_____
_____	_____	_____	_____

NOTES:

STEP 1
Floor and furniture plans: **BEDROOM 1**

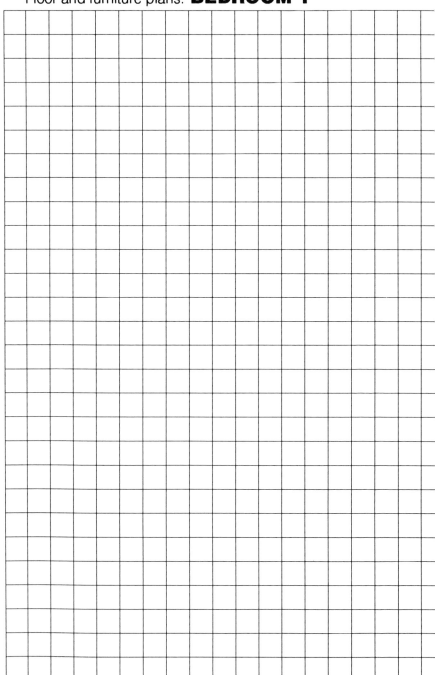

scale: 1/4 inch = 1 foc

STEP 2

BEDROOM 1

notes • ideas • photos • pictures • furniture

Type of Scheme: ❏ One color (one wedge of the color wheel)

❏ Neighboring (2 or 3 wedges side by side)

❏ Contrasting (opposite wedges)

Type of Style: ❏ Traditional, Country, Victorian

❏ Contemporary, Eclectic

===== Contacts, phone numbers, product information: =====

STEP 3
BEDROOM 1 COLOR CHART

Wall Color

Wood Trim

Ceiling

Floor Color

Tile Color

Wood or Vinyl Color

Appliance Color

Cabinet Color

Counter Color

Hardware & Accessories

Window Covering Color

Other

Furniture Wood Color

Fabric Colors

Wall Covering

Wood Trim

Ceiling

Floor Covering

Tile Piece

Wood Floor Stain or Vinyl

Hardware & Accessories

Window Fabric

Other

Furniture Stain

Main Fabric Swatch

More Fabrics

STEP 1
Measurements: **BEDROOM 2**

Length _____ x Width _____ = Square feet _____

Ceiling Height = _____

Windows	Length	Width	Depth
_____	_____	_____	_____
_____	_____	_____	_____

Doors	Length	Width	Depth
_____	_____	_____	_____
_____	_____	_____	_____

OTHER	Length	Width	Depth
_____	_____	_____	_____
_____	_____	_____	_____
_____	_____	_____	_____

NOTES:

STEP 1

Floor and furniture plans: **BEDROOM 2**

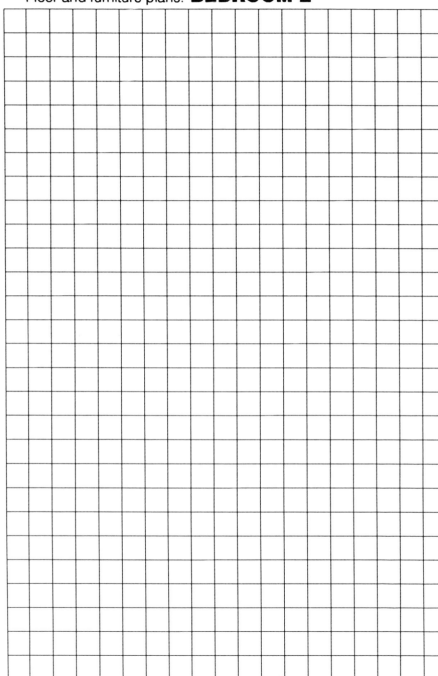

174

scale: 1/4 inch = 1 foot

STEP 2

BEDROOM 2
notes • ideas • photos • pictures • furniture

Type of Scheme: ❑ One color (one wedge of the color wheel)

❑ Neighboring (2 or 3 wedges side by side)

❑ Contrasting (opposite wedges)

Type of Style: ❑ Traditional, Country, Victorian

❑ Contemporary, Eclectic

═══ Contacts, phone numbers, product information: ═══

STEP 3
BEDROOM 2 COLOR CHART

Wall Color

Wood Trim

Ceiling

Floor Color

Tile Color

Wood or Vinyl Color

Appliance Color

Cabinet Color

Counter Color

Hardware & Accessories

Window Covering Color

Other

Furniture Wood Color

Fabric Colors

Wall Covering

Wood Trim

Ceiling

Floor Covering

Tile Piece

Wood Floor Stain or Vinyl

Hardware & Accessories

Window Fabric

Other

Furniture Stain

Main Fabric Swatch

More Fabrics

STEP 1
Measurements: **BEDROOM 3**

Length _____ x Width _____ = Square feet _____

Ceiling Height = _____

Windows	Length	Width	Depth
_____	_____	_____	_____
_____	_____	_____	_____

Doors	Length	Width	Depth
_____	_____	_____	_____
_____	_____	_____	_____

OTHER	Length	Width	Depth
_____	_____	_____	_____
_____	_____	_____	_____
_____	_____	_____	_____

NOTES:

STEP 1
Floor and furniture plans: **BEDROOM 3**

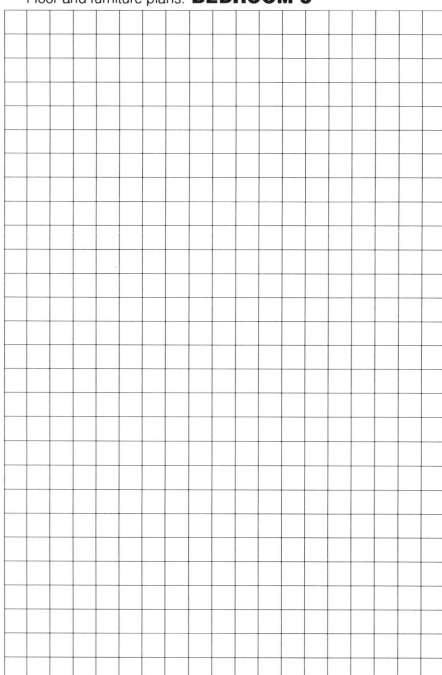

scale: 1/4 inch = 1 foot

STEP 2

BEDROOM 3
notes • ideas • photos • pictures • furniture

Type of Scheme: ❑ One color (one wedge of the color wheel)

❑ Neighboring (2 or 3 wedges side by side)

❑ Contrasting (opposite wedges)

Type of Style: ❑ Traditional, Country, Victorian

❑ Contemporary, Eclectic

═══ Contacts, phone numbers, product information: ═══

STEP 3
BEDROOM 3 COLOR CHART

Wall Color

Wood Trim

Ceiling

Floor Color

Tile Color

Wood or Vinyl Color

Appliance Color

Cabinet Color

Counter Color

Hardware & Accessories

Window Covering Color

Other

Furniture Wood Color

Fabric Colors

Wall Covering

Wood Trim

Ceiling

Floor Covering

Tile Piece

Wood Floor Stain or Vinyl

Hardware & Accessories

Window Fabric

Other

Furniture Stain

Main Fabric Swatch

More Fabrics

STEP 1

Measurements: **BATHROOM 2**

Length _____ x Width _____ = Square feet _____

Ceiling Height = _____

Bath Fixtures	Length	Width	Depth
tub/shower	_____	_____	_____
toilet	_____	_____	_____
sink	_____	_____	_____

Cabinets	Length	Width	Depth
_____	_____	_____	_____
_____	_____	_____	_____

Counter Tops	Length	Width	Depth
_____	_____	_____	_____
_____	_____	_____	_____

Windows	Length	Width	Depth
_____	_____	_____	_____
_____	_____	_____	_____

Doors	Length	Width	Depth
_____	_____	_____	_____
_____	_____	_____	_____

Other	Length	Width	Depth
_____	_____	_____	_____
_____	_____	_____	_____
_____	_____	_____	_____

NOTES:

STEP 1
Floor and furniture plans: **BATHROOM 2**

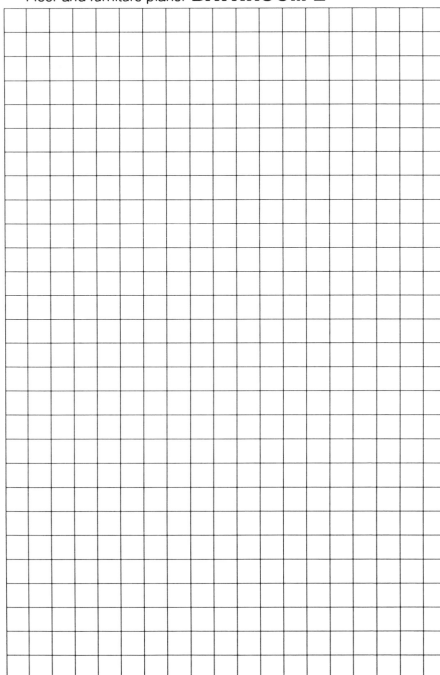

scale: 1/4 inch = 1 foot

STEP 2
BATHROOM 2
notes • ideas • photos • pictures • furniture

Type of Scheme: ❑ One color (one wedge of the color wheel)

❑ Neighboring (2 or 3 wedges side by side)

❑ Contrasting (opposite wedges)

Type of Style: ❑ Traditional, Country, Victorian

❑ Contemporary, Eclectic

═══ Contacts, phone numbers, product information: ═══

STEP 3
BATHROOM 2 COLOR CHART

Wall Color	Wood Color	Ceiling Color
Floor Color	Tile Color	Counter Color
Sink/Tub Color	Cabinets	Window Cover Color
Shower Curtain Color	Hardware Color	Other
	Accessories	

Wall Covering

Wood Trim

Ceiling

Floor Tile Piece

Wall Tile Piece

Counter Top

Sink

Toilet

Tub

Window Cover

Shower Curtain

Hardware

Other & Accessories

STEP 1

Measurements: _____ **ROOM**

Length _____ x Width _____ = Square feet _____

Ceiling Height = _____

Appliances	Length	Width	Depth
_____	_____	_____	_____
_____	_____	_____	_____
_____	_____	_____	_____

Cabinets	Length	Width	Depth
_____	_____	_____	_____
_____	_____	_____	_____

Counter Tops	Length	Width	Depth
_____	_____	_____	_____
_____	_____	_____	_____

Windows	Length	Width	Depth
_____	_____	_____	_____
_____	_____	_____	_____

Doors	Length	Width	Depth
_____	_____	_____	_____
_____	_____	_____	_____

Other	Length	Width	Depth
_____	_____	_____	_____
_____	_____	_____	_____
_____	_____	_____	_____

NOTES:

STEP 1

Floor and furniture plans: _____ **ROOM**

scale: 1/4 inch = 1 foot

STEP 2

_____ ROOM
notes • ideas • photos • pictures • furniture

Type of Scheme: ❑ One color (one wedge of the color wheel)

❑ Neighboring (2 or 3 wedges side by side)

❑ Contrasting (opposite wedges)

Type of Style: ❑ Traditional, Country, Victorian

❑ Contemporary, Eclectic

═══ Contacts, phone numbers, product information: ═══

STEP 3
_____ ROOM COLOR CHIP CHART

Wall Color	Wood Trim	Ceiling
Floor Color	Tile Color	Wood or Vinyl Color
Appliances Color	Cabinet Color	Counter Color

Sink Color   Hardware & Accessories

Window Covering Color   Other

Furniture Wood Color   Fabric Color

Wall Covering

Wood Trim

Ceiling

Floor Covering

Tile Piece

Wood Floor Stain or Vinyl

Appliance Color

Cabinet Finish

Counter Top Sample

Sink Color

Hardware & Accessories

Window Fabric

Other

Furniture Stain

Fabric Swatch

EXTERIOR

**Follow steps 1 – 4 as you did
for the interior rooms**

STEP 1
EXTERIOR MEASUREMENTS

Length _____ x Width _____ = Square feet _____

Windows	Length	Width
_____	_____	_____
_____	_____	_____
_____	_____	_____
_____	_____	_____
_____	_____	_____
_____	_____	_____

Doors	Length	Width
Front	_____	_____
Back	_____	_____
Garage	_____	_____

Porch	Length	Width	Depth
Front	_____	_____	_____
Back	_____	_____	_____

Other

_____	_____	_____	_____
_____	_____	_____	_____

NOTES:

Roof Covering

Landscape

Brick Piece

Vinyl

Other

Front Door Stain

Wood Trim Stain

Gutters

Downspouts

Garage Door

Hardware & Accessories

FURNITURE TEMPLATES

(Trace over them or create your own on index cards.
Cut them out and use them to experiment with different furniture
arrangements on the graph paper floor plans for each room.)

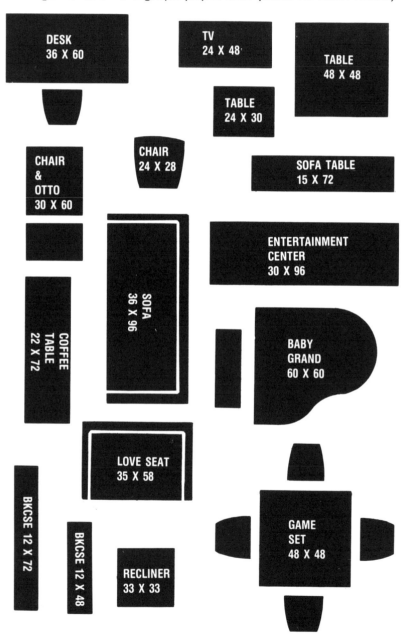

DESK
36 X 60

TV
24 X 48

TABLE
48 X 48

TABLE
24 X 30

CHAIR
&
OTTO
30 X 60

CHAIR
24 X 28

SOFA TABLE
15 X 72

ENTERTAINMENT
CENTER
30 X 96

COFFEE
TABLE
22 X 72

SOFA
36 X 96

BABY
GRAND
60 X 60

LOVE SEAT
35 X 58

BKCSE 12 X 72

BKCSE 12 X 48

RECLINER
33 X 33

GAME
SET
48 X 48

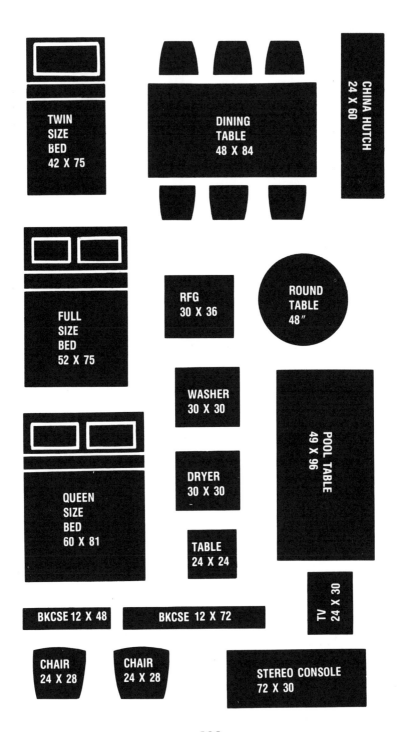

TWIN
SIZE
BED
42 X 75

DINING
TABLE
48 X 84

CHINA HUTCH
24 X 60

FULL
SIZE
BED
52 X 75

RFG
30 X 36

ROUND
TABLE
48"

WASHER
30 X 30

POOL TABLE
49 X 96

QUEEN
SIZE
BED
60 X 81

DRYER
30 X 30

TABLE
24 X 24

TV
24 X 30

BKCSE 12 X 48

BKCSE 12 X 72

CHAIR
24 X 28

CHAIR
24 X 28

STEREO CONSOLE
72 X 30

WHAT ELSE DOES THE COLOR WIZARD HAVE IN THE WORKS? AND WHAT WOULD YOU LIKE TO ASK?

Smart Home Moves® has more do-it-yourself home improvement books in the works. Each will put a smile on your face and a jingle in your pocket. Right from the Color Wizard's journal, you'll find more gems and information for making colorwize decisions, whether you're giving a room a facelift or creating a brand-new one. Whether you are buying, moving in, out, up, down or just around the same address. Watch for them, because you can't cut corners when it comes to color.

**Ask about our
seminars and workshops
for your group or organization.**

**Have any questions, ideas, or tips?
Ask The Home Color Wizard!** ℠

Order form

Making Color Work is the perfect gift for holidays, weddings, anniversaries, birthdays, housewarmings — or any other occasion.

NAME _____

ADDRESS _____

CITY _____ STATE _____ ZIP _____

PHONE _____

Number of Books _____ @ $15.95 = _____

Sales tax (6%) _____
Michigan residents only

Postage _____
($2.00 for one book,
75¢ for each additional book.)
TOTAL _____

If shipping address is different than above, please indicate here:

NAME _____

ADDRESS _____

CITY _____ STATE _____ ZIP _____

PHONE _____

Mail check or money order, payable to:

Smart Home Moves
P.O. Box 104
St. Clair Shores, MI 48080

Please allow 4-6 weeks for delivery.